The Music Career You Don't Have... *Yet.*

10 Cutting Edge Secrets
Plus a Powerfully Proven System
I Use To Earn $15,000+ Each Month.

David Paul Ruttenberg

Copyright & Disclosures

While all attempts have been made to verify the information provided in this publication, neither the author, nor the publisher assumes any responsibility for errors, omissions, or contrary interpretations on the subject matter herein.

This book is for entertainment purposes only. The views expressed are those of the author alone, and should not be taken as expert instruction or commands. **The reader is responsible for his or her own actions.**

A few affiliate links may be included throughout these pages. All products recommended have been personally used and/or tested by the author. Readers or purchasers are advised to do their own research before making any purchases. **Again, the reader is responsible for his or her own purchases and actions.**

Table of Contents

Foreword

Welcome to what I hope will be the start of a rewarding adventure.

Should your experience turn out to be anything like mine, you will have many wonderful journeys ahead of you.

While you may be a beginner in the music and/or entertainment industry, please know that *everyone*—at one time or another (and especially me!)—had to start *somewhere*. I can assure you that if this is the case with your life, you'll be just fine.

Even if you happen to be *anywhere* along the continuum of those gainfully employed, from just starting out to a global success story, I'm hoping that you *too* will find some useful nuggets about navigating other careers that are available to you.

Yes, seasoned professionals have confirmed that many of the strategies listed inside these pages are refreshing, purposeful, and productive.

Perhaps most importantly, I want to mention the following:

I'm hoping that once you put this book down, you'll not only get into action using the strategies listed, but you'll share your experiences and successes with me.

To do this, you can find me online at davidruttenberg.com or at MusiCareers.com. Please don't be shy; you can also drop me a line at hello@MusiCareers.com and join any number of my online social groups like our Blog, Facebook, Twitter (or @HiMusiCareers), YouTube, LinkedIn, Google+, Pinterest, and Reddit.

When I write that I "hope" you will be in touch—I'll go a step further than every other author out there. I'm going to ask you to **call me on the telephone** if you want to hire me for my mentoring, coaching, or consulting services. My rates are reasonable, and I'd love to help you out.

You can call me any time at:

+1 (415) 723-0562

Lastly, I'd like to thank a few people who have made this first of a series of e-books possible:

To my wife Suzy and our daughter Phoebe, thanks for providing me the environment, support, and love to do what I enjoy most. Without being able to help others and make a contribution to their lives, I would not be able to enjoy the two of you. I love you both dearly.

To my immediate family Paul, Rochelle, and Sharon Ruttenberg—thanks for putting up with all of my "noise" as a child and for supporting my education with love, encouragement, and wisdom. Without you, I would never know the joys of music and the unconditional love of parents and a sister.

To the extended family—including Seth Schreiber, Jesse Greenberg, Stuart, Karyn, and Joseph Grossman, The Lang Families, The Cousin Club, and all of my dearest friends who have become extended family...thank you for your genuine love and support. My circle (of which you are all a part) is small, but the love is genuine and enormous. It gets no better.

To University of Miami Professor Emeritus, author, and consulting engineer Ken Pohlmann—who mentored, guided, and networked me to my first real gig in the industry...I thank you. My success would not be possible without your sage guidance, kindness, and willingness to extend yourself beyond the classroom. From the bottom of my heart, I thank you immensely.

To the late Herman Emerson Meyers and George Steiner of Catholic University and The George Washington Universities, respectively—I am indebted to you both. Without you two, my foray into electronic music would never have begun. You were mavericks, both educationally and artistically, and your free thinking enabled the launch of GWU's first electronic music laboratory and studios. I thank you both and pray you rest in peace.

To my editor, the great Jean Hall—I want to express my heartfelt appreciation for your expertise, encouragement, and friendship.

Working with you has been delightful, educational and enjoyable. Without your assistance, this book would be incomplete. Thank you so very much.

And finally, to my daughter's faithful service dog and studio puppy Dulce—you're the best foot-warmer and writing companion I could ever have. You have truly made a difference in the lives of a little girl and her family, and I love you for all of this and so much more.

How To Use This Book

Be certain to read Chapter 1—in particular, the second sub-chapter entitled "Who This Book *Is Not* For." If you're in a hurry, you have my permission to skip over Chapter 2, which is about my background. There's no ego on my part; you can return to it at a later date if you want to see how I made my careers in the music and entertainment industry happen.

I would, however, strongly urge you to review the section in Chapter 2 entitled "How I Can Help You..." And for all of Chapter 3, you may want to keep a pen, pad of paper, tablet, or computer nearby to take some notes.

If you're reading the e-book, don't forget to mark up the text with an electronic highlighter. Create a set of notecards listing the actionable items you can work on when you've finished reading. Email the cards to yourself, and get to work.

Don't be afraid to skip around and focus on what you perceive to be the most applicable information to your specific needs. You know your objectives better than anyone else. I truly believe that the educational, strategic, and networking ideas conveyed in this book will line up with your aspirations.

Make certain that you also take advantage of the social, online, and personal ways to reach out to me. Just in case you missed it, you can always connect to me using any of the following links, specifically:

- Visit me online at davidruttenberg.com or at MusiCareers.com.
- You can always email me at hello@MusiCareers.com or call me to schedule mentoring services for reasonable fees at +1 (415) 723-0562. Yes...that's my direct telephone number.
- Read more at my blog, or connect with me on Facebook.
- Tweet me at Twitter (or @HiMusiCareers).
- Watch the latest MusiCareer.com videos on YouTube.
- Send me your professional listing on LinkedIn.
- Find out more about MusiCareers on Google+, Pinterest, and Reddit.

I look forward to connecting with you personally—and often.

Chapter 1
How Did You Get Here?

"Don't reinvent the wheel — just realign it."
- *Anthony J. D'Angelo*

What Is Your Goal?

So—how did you get here? What's your goal?

Maybe you're a musician and have been trying to get regular gigs at local establishments. You've been struggling because the pay stinks, and the jobs are few and far between.

Maybe you're a composer, lyricist, singer-songwriter, and you've attempted to get published. You've found the agreements you've been pursuing haven't amounted to much. It could be that you have not received any offers at all.

Or maybe you're in a band that's produced demos, an EP, or a full-length album. Still, not one major label (or independent) has offered you the record contract you so desperately covet.

You might even be a professional currently employed in the music or entertainment industry...and you're not happy, wondering if the grass is greener at another job.

Whatever your station in life, whatever your experience—my fervent hope is to make a contribution to you...right now, today! I want to make a difference by helping you get to where you want to be.

In order to accomplish this, I have to immediately suggest that you stop your current efforts and think differently about what it means to make a decent living (and not a meager one).

Far too many of my customers are hell-bent on starving in the name of their craft. I do not want this for them, and I certainly don't want it for you.

My intention is to make a significant contribution to you whereby you will never have to work a second or third job in order to practice your craft. I want your *first* love of music to be the stepping stone to a *singular career* that can support you, your family, and your lifestyle.

At the same time, I'm going to request—no matter how you show up at this point in your life—that you honor my strategies listed on these pages by thinking *outside of your current view*.

By "thinking outside," I mean this:

- If you are a musician, vocalist, singer/songwriter, or performer looking for a record deal—you *think broadly about other employment possibilities*.

- If you're a composer, lyricist, or arranger looking for a publisher—you also *think more expansively about other opportunities* to earn a salary.

- And if you're a gig musician who wants to play 15,000-seat arenas—I ask you also to approach this book with an open mind. You, too, will need to *think about other solutions* that provide earning potential.

And yes, if you're currently employed in the industry—you'll need to think about other options to making a meaningful contribution and earning a decent salary in our industries.

If you're still here and will honor my request to remain open to possibilities, opportunities, and alternatives—I believe I can get you to where you want to be.

Are you ready?

Who This Book *Is Not* For

Let me be clear about one thing—I am not going to provide you with education, strategy, or networking tips if you are seeking a career as a performing musician, vocalist, band, or singer-songwriter.

There are far too many books, articles, and resources that offer this type of information. Most of these, I believe, are not terribly useful or capable of providing you with the results you seek.

It's not that I don't believe in you, or that I don't think you are capable of achieving these objectives. You may have the talent, ambition, and ability to succeed in this sector of the music and entertainment business.

However—and from my experience—this performance segment is entirely too "congested." More to the point: The "availability" for new artists to earn a significant salary is extremely limited.

For these two reasons (congestion and availability), I would respectfully suggest you look elsewhere.

On the other hand, if you truly believe you were put here on this earth to perform and that your destiny is to become the next Super Group, Mega-Artist, etc.—then please, put this book down and seek advice elsewhere.

Why?

Because I really do want you to succeed. However, I know my limitations. And I do not feel positive about being able to help you navigate this career path.

For similar reasons, I would humbly suggest that if you're a composer, songwriter, lyricist—or anyone who is interested in a publishing deal—please look to another book, article, or resource.

While less crowded than the performing space mentioned above, the competition for new participants in the industry is fierce. As a result, I respectfully encourage you to pursue your dream elsewhere. You are better off stopping now and closing this book.

And finally, if you are hell-bent on seeking the limelight and stage 300+ nights a year in front of capacity crowds, well—by now, you know my position:

Put this book down.

To be perfectly clear: It's not that I don't believe in you or your abilities, your passion, your creativity, your stage presence, or your drive.

It is a statistical nightmare, one that I've seen few people successfully navigate and obtain a sustainable career that I could replicate with ease for others.

That being said, if you're willing to broaden your horizon, I believe I can help you practice your craft, remain in the music industry, and make a decent living while achieving happiness and fulfillment.

Are you *really* ready?

Chapter 2
Who Am I,
Where It All Began,
And How Can I Help You?

"Walking with a friend in the dark
is better than walking alone in the light."
— *Helen Keller*

A Bit About Me

From a 35,000-foot vantage point: You might be interested to learn that I have been and/or continue to be one of the following in the music and entertainment industries:

- Musician
- Vice President of Sales
- Regional Marketing Manager
- Advertising Sales Manager
- Publisher
- .com Entrepreneur
- Technical and Legal Consultant
- GRAMMY Producer
- AFM Recording Engineer/Mixer
- BMI Composer/Arranger/Publisher
- Instructor
- Lecturer
- Mentor, and
- Author

So how did this all happen, and where did I start?

Before we get into the nitty gritty...the "bit about me" that follows is actually a very comprehensive re-telling of my heritage in the music and entertainment industry.

It's hardly a "bit" at all.

In truth, I provide some gruesome details about some of my careers and the truisms I learned along the way. Many of these axioms still benefit me, my customers, and my proteges to this day.

So if you're interested, please read on.

But if you'd rather dive into the **10 Essential Steps**—please feel free to do so now, and skip ahead to Chapter 3. You can always return to this chapter for some additional "pearls of wisdom."

Even More Details About Me...

And now, it is time for the nitty-gritty. No more views from way up high. Let's get into the details.

Welcome to South Florida in the early 1960s. I grew up in a modest home with a tight-knit family, located in the suburbs.

I did not come from a family of musicians, nor was anyone I knew allied to the music or entertainment industries.

At age three, I just happened to stumble upon an electric organ—and subsequently, piano.

As a toddler turned elementary-grade student then middle-schooler (we called it junior high school back in the day), I pursued non-stop, classical piano training with private instructors at a local university/conservatory.

By the time I was 13, I was playing in regular gig-bands, earning decent money for someone my age. Disco was the rage back then, and we mixed in Top-40, jazz, and standards at our regular club dates.

Those performances at weddings, conventions, and corporate affairs were a great learning experience. In particular, I realized that performing night after night wasn't my "thing." I did not crave the stage, and the monotony of performing the same songs over and over in front of crowds large and small didn't do anything for me.

Off to College

After graduating high school, I took a break from performing and from music lessons. I went off to a university in the Northeastern United States to study everything—except music. I took a complete break for one solid academic year. And you know what?

I missed music.

So, during my second year at the university, I decided to further my musical studies. The only problem was this: the university didn't have a school of music. While they had a "department," fewer than 20 students were enrolled there.

But the university did have a great department leader who took the time to get to know me. He permitted me to express my desire to fuse music and electronics into some type of curriculum. In the end, he suggested that I create my own course of study— interspersed with the general music courses that his small team of departmental professors offered.

Of greater significance, the departmental chair brought on staff one of the patriarchs of the electronic music genre. This particular professor's connection to the art, combined with his influence and mentorship, was priceless.

Together, he and I constructed a new, world-class electronic music studio in the basement of a newly built academic study hall. He exposed me to the classic techniques of the genre, along with a technical smattering of all that he knew.

Best of all, we socialized outside of the classroom. I felt I had connected with one of the greatest teachers in my short time on this planet.

As I wound down my sophomore year, I realized that while the educational outlook was tremendous, the career prospects for an electronic music performer or composer were not that great. The research I came upon (particularly as it related to employment) was neither positive nor promising.

Off To College, Part Deux

While the professorial and student relationships I carved out were extremely rewarding, I ultimately transferred to another university, to start over by better defining my "end game."

In so doing, I returned to South Florida and to the institution where I had previously studied classical piano. However, this time, I was determined to graduate—but not with a degree in performance, composition, theory, etc.

Rather, I was determined to earn a degree leading to a job that fused my love of music, electronics, and business. This would be one that would put food on the table and a roof over my head...

I learned a valuable and important lesson about "Defining Your Goals" in my collegiate transfer process. This will apply to your search for the right career, and I detail it in RULE #1 in the chapter that follows.

In the end, I graduated with a nifty degree from the second university... after creating the first regular undergraduate newsletter and joining the School of Music's Honor Society. I also created additional "deliverables," including professional audio equipment reviews for an international trade magazine.

Before graduating, I also founded and became president of the university's premiere Audio Engineering Society Chapter. There, I was responsible for raising capital finance and scheduling a world-renowned lecturer to speak at our school (among other activities). I also provided scholarship assistance to students who wouldn't otherwise be able to afford attending international conventions, exhibitions, and white papers.

All the while, I was able to network (and help others network), connecting to industry veterans and professionals in pursuit of post-collegiate careers (i.e., high-paying jobs).

There was a slight detour prior to having my degree conferred. It was not entirely unexpected. In fact, while most deviations can be perceived as negative, this was far from that.

A Detour Defined
In my junior year at the university, I had begun to interview (ostensibly for summer internships) with several major professional audio manufacturing organizations. My professors gave me recommendations to meet with companies like Dolby, Phillips/Dupont Optical, NEOTEK Audio Consoles, and General Motors Photographic.

Each of these meetings required leaving school, getting on airplanes, and attending lengthy interview and testing procedures. It was, to say the least, exciting.

Ultimately, I was offered a full-time position (not merely a summer internship) at NEOTEK Corporation. Specifically, I was to serve as the company's vice president of sales and marketing, and I was asked to start immediately. All at the tender age of 22, and in the middle of my junior year of college.

And no, I had not yet marched in graduation exercises. I had no cap and gown to show for my efforts—and I was determined to have both the job *and* my diploma.

Clearly, this presented a wonderful opportunity; however, it was critical to me that I finish my classes so that a degree could be conferred. In the end, here's what happened:

- The university's dean, administrators, and my dear professors/mentors were beyond helpful in suggesting solutions that were forward-thinking and benefited all parties.
- The School of Music was able to lay claim to having one— if not the youngest—vice president in professional audio manufacturing as a recent graduate, provided that I complete my coursework while in Chicago and come back to teach three master classes over the following twelve months.
- The employer got a new, eager, and energized employee.

- I was able to have one foot firmly in academia, leading to a conferred degree, while with the other, earning experience, gratitude, and a paycheck throughout my senior year of college.

Before telling you how it all ended up...don't forget to check out Step #5 in the "Ten Essential Steps" Chapter that follows. The concept of using "Deliverables" is a huge secret weapon that landed me this job and can help in your career advancement as well.

Now, back to the story...

I relocated to Chicago to start my first big career in the music industry. My job was to focus on audio recording console design, sales, installation, and servicing for artist, film, TV, and broadcast studios. I landed in a fancy apartment, had a great 9–5 job, and traveled every other month to great venues across the country.

Chicago Boss Bust

Just as everything was settling into a groove, a major disaster occurred at work.

My brand-new Chicago boss—the sole owner and chief executive officer of the company—was accused of *allegedly* having multiple affairs with employees inside the organization. This created a less-than-stellar office environment and culture, particularly since one of the employees was a direct reporter to my position.

Within weeks following my arrival, it became abundantly apparent that several employees would be taking legal action...and I did not want to be a witness, let alone a party, to any court proceedings that might be scheduled.

Fortunately, and not long after morale at the company began to nosedive, I received a telephone call from an executive search firm in California. They called looking to fill a new position that, while it ultimately would be based in Chicago, required an immediate relocation to San Francisco for training.

The San Francisco company was the United States headquarters for a well-respected Japanese manufacturer of analog and digital tape recorders. They had also captured a large percentage of the video duplication and manufacturing markets.

It was an interesting opportunity at a company that had a much broader product offering and a larger footprint in the industry. There were also considerably greater sales channels as well as penetration that far exceeded my first job opportunity in Chicago.

On the plane ride back from my interview in San Francisco, I realized what an excruciatingly difficult decision lay ahead of me. The issues were primarily threefold:

1. From a resume perspective, I did not want it to appear that I could not maintain job continuity right out of college. Leaving my first career after only a few months could, after all, be perceived as a "red flag" to future employers.
2. I had negotiated an arrangement with my university (remember—I had still *not* graduated), and my

commencement was based on completing work while at my Chicago job. I did not want to jeopardize my commitment to the dean, administrators, or my professors/mentors. I wanted to obtain my degree...even though I was already gainfully employed in the "business."

3. I also did not want to complicate my relationship with my initial Chicago employer. After all, he had given me the opportunity to leave the university early and start my career as an audio professional. While he allegedly put himself, his business, and all his employees at risk—I *did* benefit because of his trust, his job offer, and his willingness to do something nice for me.

Life Works Its Way Out

As is often the case with troubling situations like these—life always has a way of working itself out.

My authenticity and honesty during my San Francisco interview earned me a second job. The California firm provided tremendous support in migrating to my new home while retaining my Chicago residency for the future.

Yes...you read that accurately.

They paid for everything. Two moves (to San Francisco and then back to Chicago). Two apartments (one to hold for my return and another great flat at the top of Nob Hill in downtown San Francisco)!

Better still, I was offered a very healthy California-cost-of-living "raise" that represented a major increase over my previous Chicago salary.

Not surprisingly, my university fully supported my decision to leave Chicago, given the troubling legal circumstances. Furthermore, because other graduates were already employed by the San Francisco company, the university was more than happy to announce that I was receiving a promotion of sorts in a lateral industry move.

In fact, while the position was predominantly domestic-based (rather than international in scope like my previous Chicago position), the equipment and services line was considerably broader and more prestigious.

Best of all, I never experienced any ill-will or criticism from my former Chicago firm, its employees or, most surprisingly, my first boss.

From time to time, I would run into him at conventions, meetings, and trade shows, and—at least to me—he was always *extremely* professional, courteous, and encouraging.

So, with this portion of my career, a few important lesson emerged from this "disaster":

- Integrity is critical at *every* stage of one's career.
- Remain honest and grateful, and *acknowledge* those who have helped you.
- Do your best to be *authentic* in every moment.

- Have the *courage* to create a positive outcome.

The above bullets form critical personality attributes that you must exercise to increase your success on the job. They are the backbone of RULE #3 in the following section entitled "How Can I Help You?" and should not be overlooked.

I never thought my California job could be topped. The people at my company, our manufacturer representatives, dealers, and customers, were some of the most intelligent, creative, and fun people to work with. It was a "heady" time in the industry as the move from analog to digital tape recording was in full swing.

Larger-format audio consoles required larger and larger tape machines that could be synchronized to create super-recording rigs of 96+ channels of audio. Sound for video and film-post became a critical market segment as surround sound and digital displays became commonplace.

And then, on Monday, October 19, 1987, something awful occurred.

Black Monday.

Market Collapse

This was *the* day that caused worldwide panic among financial markets. What started that morning in Hong Kong and spread to Europe eventually hit the United States and the Dow Jones Industrial Average by midmorning. Hauntingly, this occurred almost 58 years to the day of the initial stock market crash of 1929.

Specifically, the market experienced a massive decline, giving back nearly 23% of its entire value. Think of it this way: Every dollar invested lost nearly 1/4 of its principal. This was a mammoth loss. A complete wipe-out.

More importantly, our San Francisco company always paid US cash for products made by our Japanese parent company. With the decline in the market, the yen-to-dollar exchange rate made it difficult for us to obtain new products. Essentially, our costs nearly doubled; moreover, the costs to our customers quadrupled.

Picture this:

1. You're a recording, TV, film, or broadcast studio, and you need new tape-recording equipment.
2. The amount of money you had in your accounts has just decreased by nearly 25% because of the market crash. The value of your company, if you were a publicly traded concern, dropped as well.
3. The budget you were initially allotted for new tape machines has been cut by 2/3. You now can only purchase 33% of the machines you *desperately* need.
4. And to make matters worse, the machines now cost 4x the amount you were originally quoted.

Guess what happened?

Sales at our California company tanked. The industry fell into a malaise. Layoffs abounded, and long-time employees were terminated.

In my case, I was offered a position back in San Francisco that would require me to pull up stakes in Chicago and say goodbye to my Midwestern professional network. After years in the Midwest, I had forged a great personal life that—quite frankly—I was not ready to dismiss.

So—guess what?

You Ought To Be In Magazines

The same executive search firm that had hired me from Chicago to San Francisco came to my rescue. This time, they hired and found me another position in an allied career to the music and entertainment industry: *business-to-business magazines*.

My new firm was based in Kansas but had offices near my apartment in Chicago. A relocation to Kansas wasn't required (although quite a bit of travel was).

Best of all, I landed the job because, unlike most of my sales associates who had only magazine and communication backgrounds, my direct knowledge about music manufacturing and the entertainment industry (e.g., my command of all types of studio equipment and more) applied to my new magazine customers. These were predominantly Midwestern manufacturers who required editorial coverage and advertising in our two leading publications.

It was an awesome job, selling an intangible set of products and services that did not fluctuate based on exchange rates. Too, magazine readership (prior to the internet) was a growing concern. Our two magazines did well in both the recording studio and the commercial sound and video contracting industries. In fact, we were number two and number one against the competition.

It's worth mentioning that prior to making my move to the Kansas firm, I received my degree from the university—after fulfilling my responsibilities to the dean, the administrators, and my professors. One of my proudest days came during my graduation exercise back in Florida. Regrettably, I couldn't stay long as I was due at business meetings in both Chicago *and* New York the following day.

Thus, I flew back to my job and settled into a routine of getting to work early, finishing my assignments expeditiously, collecting a nice salary and bonuses, and traveling around the country, servicing my customers and company.

During this time, and in spite of a pretty rigorous business travel schedule, I put down deeper roots in Chicago and eventually found a partner, became engaged, and married. As she was an airline employee, we combined our travels and met up for lunches and dinners outside our home city—when we weren't working.

Stupid Is as Stupid Does

And... in one idiotic and insanely stupid move, I foolishly turned in a travel expense report requesting reimbursement for air travel that had been paid for using a complimentary airline ticket affiliated with my spouse's employer.

I'm fairly certain this wasn't a simple oversight on my part. Looking back, I probably thought it was an easy way to make a few extra dollars (less than $150, to be exact).

I can't honestly rationalize such a stupid move. One thing is for certain: There was absolutely no reason to do this as I was making a healthy salary and bonuses.

After the reimbursement was denied, I received a call from my boss in Kansas inquiring about this airline ticket issue. Of course, I immediately confessed to my failings. And, with his call, I knew that would be my last full day of employment at the company.

The next morning, about 30 minutes after I arrived in the office (to finish packing my personal belongings), my boss appeared in the doorway to walk me out of the building. He and I were actually great friends (though, regrettably, he is now no longer living). He mentioned he was genuinely saddened to see me leave. Moreover, he was very surprised that I was already packed and ready to depart when he arrived.

With that, I took a lonely cab ride back to our apartment and learned that my stroke of bad news was just beginning. My epic-career fail was followed by the impending failure of my marriage.

Worse still, we had only just returned from our honeymoon three months earlier.

Despite the fact I made multiple appointments and attended marriage counseling/therapy sessions by myself, my spouse refused to attend. As my therapist suggested, "Your bride simply does not have the 'sea legs' to work through your difficulties."

As a result, within 45 days, we had abandoned our efforts, moved our separate ways, and I returned to Florida to file for divorce.

Whatever you do, don't skip RULE #4 in the following section. *Karma* has a funny way of surfacing just when you need a tremendous "life lesson." You'll see what I mean, next.

Going Back to Miami

It was a pretty depressing time. As I was no longer gainfully employed in the industries I loved, music and entertainment took a major sabbatical from my career plan.

While in Florida, I contended with the mess I had made of my life. With the help of a great family (both immediate and extended) and wonderful friends, the relocation gave way to a rebirth with amazing new chapters about to unfold.

While relying on my electrical engineering degree and computer science skills, I began servicing computer networks for professional associations (e.g., physicians, attorneys, and other similar offices).

Around the same time and a few years before the birth of the Netscape browser, a high school friend turned computer consultant approached me to join forces and create a new type of consulting company.

The Birth of a .com Business

Graced by the unmatched abilities, fearlessness, and genius of my new girlfriend, the three of us launched the third largest internet consultancy in the Southeastern United States. We provided digital and traditional marketing services (think radio, TV, print, and internet advertising) to the Fortune 100.

We grew in size to employ contractors on three continents as we serviced huge organizations and teamed with even larger advertising and public relations firms. Our company brought dozens of institutions like Sony Music, Blockbuster, DirecTV, Goodyear Tire and Rubber, and several hotel chains to the internet *and* the traditional media world.

We relocated our business three times during our nearly 10-year run. Each time, we acquired hipper, more cutting-edge workspaces that—combined with our nascent but "fast-company" growth—made us the darlings of the marketplace.

Along the way, we were eyed for merger and acquisition deals by those who had larger dreams and even bigger wallets. We did well during the early "dot com" years.

Just as my business life was experiencing an upswing, so was my personal world. My company's chief executive officer and co-founder and my girlfriend eventually became my fiancée and then my spouse.

Soulmates to the End of Time
Today, the love of my life, Suzy Girard-Ruttenberg, and I have worked, traveled, and made a difference in others' lives for more than 26 years. We built a very comfortable existence in Florida, and we have traveled the world.

Suzy is also the mother of our delightful red-headed daughter Phoebe; undoubtedly our magnum opus.

Too, Suzy is a world-class entrepreneur. Put succinctly, Suzy is the most fearless, brilliant, confident, and capable business leader, corporate coach, and social change operative I know.

So what ever happened to our internet business?

Toward the turn of the century, and despite our intense growth, I missed my careers in the music and entertainment industries.

Combined with the tragic death of close family members—along with the events of 9/11—I began to focus on the importance of making real contributions to others. Ultimately, creating "pretty websites and advertising campaigns" wasn't my ultimate objective.

With the assistance of a business coach and my CEO/wife's unflinching support, I left (and eventually helped to wind down) our internet consultancy.

I then "retired" at the tender age of 40.

Mind you, I didn't stop working. I just retired from the ".com business."

Entrepreneurial Gig, Part Deux

After a few false starts attempting to re-enter the entrepreneurial space, I realized that no one was out there helping others "demystify" the music industry from three perspectives:

- *Enjoying the process* of mastering musical instruments and voice;
- Harnessing the power of the computer to bring music production to *talented but unskilled artists*; and
- Providing composition, production, and record deliverables to talent who didn't know *how to release their music.*

So I designed and built a custom studio in our home, marketed to the local community, and within 24 months had over 150 customers in both group and private appointments, 6 days a week.

The "music/vocal instruction" side of the business accounted for nearly 80% of my revenues, while the "production" side gave off 20% of the income. Over the last 17 years, this has flipped dramatically as more of my "former" music industry contacts learned that I had returned to this market and sought my skills.

Since becoming a GRAMMY® producer, AFM engineer/mixer, BMI composer, arranger, publisher—I've been fortunate to create a varied discography ranging the gamut of musical genres from rap to religious, pop to country, singer/songwriter to heavy metal, and jazz to rhythm and blues.

And during the last decade, I've bolted on careers as a lecturer, mentor and book author.

It's been an incredible journey, spanning 40+ years. Most of the hard work has been enjoyable and rewarding. I have tremendous gratitude for making a difference in the lives of others, seeing my contributions bring tangible results, and collecting many happy memories fulfilling others' dreams.

Contributing to others first not only sets you up for continued success, it provides rewards far beyond any tangible currency you could put in your bank account. Be certain not to miss Rule #5 in the following section.

When Brushing Your Teeth At Night...
In fact, my parents' favorite quote applies:

> **"When you brush your teeth and wash your face at the end of a long day, look into the mirror...ask yourself: 'Did I do good work, did I exercise your best effort, and did I help others?'"**

Combined with my favorite saying, "Deeds Not Words"... I think my parents were spot-on accurate.

To this day, I cherish and live by their advice.

It is my fervent hope that my efforts and good work—as well as my deeds—bring you tangible results, happiness, and fulfillment.

Here's to the contributions I can make to you.

How Can I Help You?

In the previous section, I mentioned a few pivotal moments. In this section, I'm going to provide you with five rules that, if used at the proper time, will undoubtedly serve you well.

You may recall that early in my collegiate period, I transferred from one university to another. In transferring to the second college, I discovered the most important rule for selecting a higher learning institution.

This rule applies to *any* college, university, trade school, online course, webinar, etc.

This absolutely critical rule **must** be followed if you intend to focus your career in the music and/or entertainment industries.

RULE #1: Make certain you have a clearly defined connection between your education and your ability to gain *immediate* employment following graduation.

Put even more bluntly:

You alone must determine—before even paying tuition fees or before you arrive for your first day of class—what level of tangible success your college has historically exhibited in securing real-life paying jobs for their graduates.

If your intended school, college, online class, or certification program is unable to provide you with this information — look elsewhere.

Moreover, you should request that admission officers provide you with at least five solid references of graduates you can contact directly. You want to confirm what happened to them after they graduated. Are they working in the industry?

Have coffee with them, or Skype or FaceTime with them. Ideally, you should be able to speak with dozens of graduates who are working in the business.

<u>**Without tangible proof that the degree you seek actually results in a paying job in an industry — you will be wasting your time and hard-earned money.**</u>

Remember, you are not just paying money and expending valuable time in exchange for a diploma and an education. Your ultimate return on your investment (a real job) must be crystal clear BEFORE you sign up for your first day of class.

Fortunately for me, I had done this homework prior to transferring to my second university—*not* my first (my fault).

My mistake cost me two years of tuition and time. Don't let this happen to you.

As my second university had a 100% placement success rate for all graduates the nine years prior to my arrival, I knew I had landed at a very demanding but fruitful institution when I arrived. (N.B.: the program that I attended is currently in its 41st year conferring degrees and remains equally successful.)

While at school, I learned that my career interests were not necessarily shared by my classmates. Maybe it was the way I was wired. Could it be that I simply desired something out of the ordinary?

Whatever the reason, I remember networking with people who had careers that were not on the *creative* side of the business. Despite being a musician, composer, and arranger, the *non-creative jobs* held more appeal for me.

Realizing this helped me identify another important rule when crafting a strategy to enter the industry.

RULE #2: Don't follow the crowd or common trends. Be a contrarian, and think *outside the lines* of traditional career opportunities.

This rule not only applies to specific job types but to timelines and schedules, too. Remember that I left college at the end of my junior year—not when everyone else did, which was a year later.

Too, I pursued a career—not in the creative segment of the music industry— but on the design, manufacturing, and marketing and sales side.

Exploring opportunities in different market segments proved positive for me, my employer, and my university. By being a contrarian, I have enjoyed many careers that others did not know existed, and thus, *they could not compete against me.*

Once I began practicing as a professional in the industry, by differentiating myself from other employees (both inside and outside my company), I would learn another major truth related to the golden rule.

Everyone knows the "biblical" Golden Rule from Matthew 7:12 in the New Testament. The "law of the prophets" (i.e., "Do unto others as you would have them do unto you") is powerful. This principle ensures success in life—and the business world, if practiced earnestly.

I've further incorporated the golden rule as follows:

RULE #3: Practice integrity, honesty, gratitude, authenticity, and courage in *everything* you do.

These personality characteristics are often missing in both rookie employees and seasoned professionals. Learning to govern yourself by using these attributes will not only keep you in good company, they will assure your ascent to greater careers.

Best of all, you will sleep well at night. I know that I do!

And if you should falter and not follow Rule #3, as I did during my third job in the music industry, you will undoubtedly have to come to terms with your failures. I did, and I learned many difficult lessons.

With this in mind, though, I would not have traded my failures for anything.

Why?

Ultimately, my life worked out. My resolve to honor Rule #3 was affirmed, and I continue to practice it, every moment of every day.

This brings me to the concept of *Karma*, which you may already be familiar with.

If not, know that Karma can be defined as "the sum of a person's actions in this and previous states of existence."

As it applies to careers in the music and entertainment industry (and in my life), I can testify that Karma has a most amazing way of surfacing in your life, just when you need to learn a most important lesson. Thus, this is where my next rule comes into play:

RULE #4: Karma has a funny way of surfacing in your life, particularly when you abandon your principals. When you fail to practice living the most fair and decent life — a rebalancing usually settles in. Listen to your gut and rebalance by revisiting RULE #3 above.

In my particular case, by cheating on a travel reimbursement, I paid the price by losing a highly profitable job and fantastic experiences at a great company. And for added measure, my personal life went into a tailspin, resulting in a failed marriage, relocating to a different state, and having to start over.

However—and this is an equally critical component—once I cleaned up my act and began strictly following Rule Number #3 again(!) ... an explosive and positive growth period emerged for me—one that applied to my career, as well as my personal and family life.

Please read this carefully:

Scamming and/or trying to get away with frivolous and/or unnecessary gains results in a re-balancing of your life. My suggestion: Do not deviate from being honest. Maintain the highest degree of integrity. You will sail through life more peacefully and harmoniously.

Please do as I say—not as I *used* to do.

You will thank me for it. I guarantee it.

The final important point is based on *contribution*. Donating to others first not only sets you up for continued success, it provides rewards far beyond any currency you can put in your bank account.

Contribution is a critical component of getting the job you want in the music and entertainment industries. As you will learn later, one of the greatest ways to differentiate yourself from other job candidates is to take a drastically different approach to the job interviewing process. Specifically:

Before you even apply for a job at a known employer, you need to create deliverables that are meaningful to the target company where you're seeking employment. In so doing, you are likely to attract the attention of the employer because you have created something tangible that they want—beyond a warm body to fill a particular job description.

You can also cement your employment prospects (and differentiate yourself from other applicants) by approaching the interview in a contrasting manner. Instead of using the interview to learn more how the job can help you and what is required of the company—determine how you can best make a contribution to the company, both within the confines of the job description and outside the job. What does the company hope to become in terms of the industry at large? How do they want to be perceived by their customers? Beyond the job description, what can you contribute to maximize the company's success?

Again—contribution is highly underrated and sorely needed—particularly in the music and entertainment industries.

Chapter 3
The Ten Essential Steps
to Success in the Music Industry

"We are what we repeatedly do.
Excellence, then, is not an act but a habit."
- *Will Durant*

Step #1 — Define Your Goal

Seems pretty obvious, right?

But have you ever thought *why* it is important to define your goal?

Look at it this way...

You wouldn't take a vacation or go on a road trip without determining your destination, right?

The same applies to your career.

I've seen many talented people wander through their lives, accepting whatever job comes their way, only to be mystified when they end up not enjoying their work.

Why is this?

These people did not plan their outcome—and as a result, their careers turned into a road trip, meandering this way and that. In the end, they became disappointed and disgruntled.

Please. Don't let this happen to you.

Figure out where you want to end up.

Determine—right now—what makes you happiest.

Once you do, your goal is to pursue your happiness with relentless abandon and energy. While you're at it—and of equal importance—you need to determine what you absolutely do *not* enjoy doing.

In other words: Steer clear of jobs, deliverables, and careers that match up to negative emotions.

Now, don't get me wrong...

Every occupation—and I mean *every one*—has tasks that aren't pleasant. Whether it is reports, meetings, forms, paperwork, rules, etc.—no job is immune from "drudgery." You know, the kind of tasks that get in the way of happiness.

But if you are absolutely enamored of the "fun" part of your job— then you will be able to deal with the more monotonous and less-pleasant tasks that accompany it.

Where to Begin?

If a recording contract, publishing deal, or endless nights playing in bars isn't in your future, how are you supposed to determine the best way to fit into the music and entertainment industry?

The best place to start will be by examining the two comprehensive tables that appear on the following pages.

I've performed the research for you. Table 1 reveals many career types by name, description, job scenario, and salary.

Wherever possible, I have included the information source within the "Salary" column. I encourage you to further research these sources.

After you have scoured the first table, check out Table 2. You will find the latest from the United States Department of Labor's "Quick Facts."

This table includes statistics for careers that are *allied* to the music and entertainment industries (for example, advertising, promotion, and marketing managers who incorporate original or background music with their services—or even app developers who use music, sound effects, or sound design as part of their programming).

The Department of Labor provides career "names," an annualized average salary or hourly "median pay" (from their 2016 census), what type of "entry level education" and "work experience" is required, and whether the job requires or offers training.

Of most interest are the last three columns in Table 2, which indicate the current "number of jobs" filled by employees in this category (again, for the year 2016), the ten-year "job outlook" until 2026, and finally, the estimated number of available openings listed in "employment change."

It's important to start defining your goal by reviewing these tables and making some notes regarding which listings appeal most to you.

TABLE 1.

NAME	Description	Job Scenario	Salary (Source)
A&R Administrator	Provides high-level personal and administrative support to an Artists & Repertoire Representative.	Working with an A&R representative for a record label or artist management company.	$25,000 – $65,000 + (Careers In Music)
A&R Representative	Scouts talent for record labels to sign to recording contracts.	Working for a record label or artist management company.	$25,000 – $85,000
Agent	Individual who books gigs for an artist or band/ensemble using relationships with clients such as club owners.	Working directly with an artist or an artist management company.	Usually a commission of what the artist makes at the show, around 15%. A full-time agent can make great money in this profession, with the top agents in the world making millions.
Alexander Technique Instructor (Music)	Instructor who works with musicians, showing them how to normalize levels of physical and mental tension while performing.	Usually an independent instructor.	Data is not readily available for this career, but successful clinicians can make $40,000 – $70,000+.
App Development	Music apps are exceptionally popular and always need consulting, testing, and / or development from actual musicians.	As an app developer or working with another company, either a start-up or established business.	Employed developers typically make between $80,000 – $100,000 (Mashable).

Arranging	Musical reconceptualization. Ranging from orchestrating a composer's piano score to reharmonizing a melody.	Many professional film composers have arrangers on staff to complete a score quickly. In jazz, we see people like Gordon Goodwin and Christian McBride making clever arrangements for big bands.	$20,000-$45,000 annually (Berklee College of Music Salary Guide)
Artist Manager	Negotiates business deals on behalf of the artist. Also has input on the creative and marketing ends of an artist.	Either independently or with an artist management company such as Columbia Artists Management.	Up to 50% of what the artist makes
Arts Administration	Performs tasks for an arts organization. Can be basic clerical duties or advanced grant-writing and events planning.	Working in an arts organization. Some, including major orchestras and creative venues like the Brooklyn Academy of Music, have large staffs.	Between $30,000 and $50,000, with opportunities for advancement
Audio Engineer	Production specialist concerned with how sound is manipulated, recorded, and mixed in a recording. For someone specializing in acoustic sound, please see sound /	As a freelance recording engineer, in a college/university recording studio, in a commercial recording studio, etc.	Median pay is approximately $45,000, according to audioengineeringschools.net

	acoustic engineer below.		
Blogger	A journalist, writer, or commentator who writes about a specific subject and sells products, memberships, and advertising space.	Start your own blog if you want to get paid well – writing articles for other people usually does not lend itself to a lucrative career, unless you get a job at *Rolling Stone Magazine*, for example.	$0 – $100,000+
Broadcast Engineer	Oversees the "airchain," or complete path of the a/v signal from origin to destination, for a television or radio station. Requires a background in audio engineering and knowledge in electrical engineering.	Employed by a television company or radio station, or as an independent contractor.	Average is $70,000 (Glass Door)
Business Management	Oversees day-to-day operations of a music business, including a performing arts venue, nightclub, music store.	Overseeing various businesses like record labels, clubs, performing arts centers, etc.	$45,000 – $150,000+ (higher if you are an executive director)
Church Choir Director	A minister of music, this person conducts the church choir, coordinates rehearsals, plans the choir budget, etc.	Employed in a church.	Between $20,000 – $70,000

Clinician	An expert who directs part or all of a conference about music. Common clinicians include composers, conductors, performers, educators, and music marketing specialists.	As an individual being hired to conduct seminars, lectures, clinics, etc.	Based on each individual engagement (usually can charge several thousand per clinic)
Concert Music Composer	Writes music for acoustic and electro-acoustic mediums, usually in classical or contemporary genres. Differs from commercial music compositions in that it is specifically written as a stand-alone work or as an incidental stage work (like in opera) and not as a backdrop for films, video games, or commercials.	Almost entirely freelance with payments based on royalties and commissions. Many concert music composers make their livings simultaneously in commercial music or as a higher education teacher. Some composers make money being "in-residence" with a professional ensemble.	Varies widely, depending on the status of the composer
Concert Promoter	Individual or company responsible for organizing a tour or performance. Typically reaches out to artists via an artist's manager, but this is not always the case	Working for a musical artist or for a special event for an organization (like a large charity concert).	Usually depends on the success of the show, how many tickets are sold, etc. Some concert promoters make $1,000,000+

Conductor	A director who provides visible gestures as performance instructions to an orchestra.	Although the most visible place for conductors is in an orchestra, the majority of orchestras do not pay well (although some, like the Los Angeles Philharmonic and San Diego Symphony, obviously do). Most conducting jobs are available through music colleges and institutions.	Varies widely, with some assistant conductors in major orchestras making $70,000/yr. and some widely known music directors making $600,000+
Commercial Jingle Composer	Someone who writes the background music for a commercial typically lasting anywhere from 15 seconds (standard) to one minute (long).	Usually jingle composers are freelance, but some are represented by major agencies such as Air & Edelman Associates in New York.	$100 – $8,000 per jingle
Cruise Ship Performer	Performing for extended periods of time with a band on a cruise ship.	On a cruise ship. Many musicians personally audition for cruise ship staff itself or go through an agency connecting cruise ships to musicians, like Proship.com.	$450 – $2,000 per week (Musicianwages.com)

Engraving	Taking a composer's handwritten score and engraving it into a professional computer notation program such as Finale or Sibelius.	Mostly freelance, although there is a need for expert engravers at top music publishing companies.	Around $35,000 – $45,000 annually for a full-time position (Simply Hired)
Ensemble / Music Direction	Starts and / or runs a musical ensemble, orchestra, etc. Can act as the conductor as well.	Starting a musical ensemble, like Bang On a Can or the International Contemporary Ensemble.	If you are just starting out with your own ensemble, expect many years of not making too much money. If you are the music director of a major orchestra, you could be paid into the millions.
Event Planner (Music)	Someone who plans any large-scale event involving music. Music festival, music competition, ceremony involving music, concert charity event, and more.	As an independent consultant or working with an event-planning firm.	Median is $45,000 (US News)
TV Composer	Commercial composer who works to make music as the background for film and television.	Working as a contractor with independent and major film and television studios.	Television: 30-minute episode: $2,000 – $5,000+ (Average)
TV Composer			Television: 60-minute episode: $4,000 – $10,000+ (Average)
TV Composer			Made-for-Television Movie: $15-60k

Film Composer	Commercial composer who specifically works to make music as the background for film and television.	Working as a contractor with independent and major film and television studios.	Independent Film: $4,000 – $110,000 (based on budget)
Film Composer			Major Studio film: $50,000 – $1.5 million+
Film Conductor	Conducts live musicians producing the music for a motion picture.	Working as a contractor with independent and major film studios.	At least twice the pay of a performing musician in the same session, according to the union
Foley Artist	Artist creates ambient sounds of a film or television set that were not created through the physical structure and location of the set.	Film or television set or company.	$45,000 – $60,000
Front of House Engineer	Engineer runs live mixer during a musical or theatrical production. Also responsible for managing sound team, if present.	Working for a live concert venue or independently.	$30,000 – $100,000 +
Fundraiser / Development Assistant	Works to procure donations for a music company, almost always for a 501(c)(3) nonprofit.	Working in a non-profit organization, writing applications for grants from government entities, wealthy businesses and individuals, arts organizations, etc. Also helps set up events for	Average salary for a development associate in a nonprofit is $52,000 (according to Simply Hired)

		soliciting donations.	
Higher Education Teaching	Teaching at collegiate-level university, conservatory, or liberal arts college.	Higher education Institutions.	Lecturer: $25,000 – $50,000 (Full-Time)
Higher Education Teaching	Teaching at collegiate-level university, conservatory, or liberal arts college.	Higher education Institutions.	Assistant Professor: $40,000 – $70,000; more for a top university
Higher Education Teaching	Teaching at collegiate-level university, conservatory, or liberal arts college.	Higher education Institutions.	Associate Professor: $65,000 – $90,000; more for a top university
Higher Education Teaching	Teaching at collegiate-level university, conservatory, or liberal arts college.	Higher education Institutions.	Professor: $80,000 – $150,000; more for a top university
Instrument Craftsman/Builder	Compositing disparate materials to create musical instrument.	A music instrument factory, independent music store, or a sole instrument craftsman.	$32,000 – $200,000 or more
Instrument/Product Demonstrator	Perform instruments to advertise the quality and capability of an instrument.	Selling instruments through a well-known music manufacturer.	Falls under the marketing department of a major business, which would probably pay between $60,000 – $120,000 for a full-time music marketing specialist
Instrument Sales	Works at a music store to sell instruments and associated music equipment, like bows, music	Selling instruments at a music store, such as Guitar Center.	$20,000 – $60,000

	software, and amplifiers.		
Licensing Administrator	Oversees the copyrights of specific or collection of works. Licenses music and negotiates fees for the use of the work.	In a music publishing company.	$40,000 – $50,000
Location Sound Engineer	A member of film or television crew responsible for capturing the sound made on a set, including dialogue.	Working with professional equipment on a live television set.	Average is $55,000 (Simply Hired)
Marketing: Traditional and Digital Marketing	Working with an artist, publicist, college institution, or other musical entity to effectively market their products, concerts, etc. Includes a savvy understanding in both traditional marketing methods as well as digital marketing practices, such as social media and integrative marketing.	Working as a marketing contractor or with a music group or business. Different marketing opportunities include institutional marketing, concert hall marketing, music products marketing, record label marketing, etc.	Anywhere from $25,000 – $100,000+
Mastering Engineer	A post-production audio process that transfers final mix to its ultimate storage. In the process, the engineer enhances the sound using advanced software and hardware.	Mostly freelance	Salaries: $500 – $1,500 are typical fees per album mastered. $100 – $300 per individual single or track.

Military Band Performer	Performs music in a military band. Most military bands exist in the US, but there are good ones that exist overseas as well.	Employment in a professional military band.	In the United States Air Force Band, starting pay is $2,380 per month, in addition to housing and food allowances. A portion of the salary, as well as the housing and food allowances, are tax-free.
Mixing Engineer	Music production expert responsible for blending the tracks and elements of a musical recording. A specialized version of the "Audio Engineer."	As a freelance recording engineer, in a college/university recording studio, in a commercial recording studio, etc.	Many mixing engineers also take on other aspects of a music production project, like recording and sometimes mastering. The salary can vary widely based on clientele and status, but the average, according to Simply Hired, is $47,000.
Musical Theatre Artist	An artist who combines songs, dialogue, acting, and dancing to create a unique performance in this popular music genre.	Broadway companies, off-Broadway companies, and in companies throughout the country.	Salaries: Actor's Equity Union for Broadway productions is approximately $1,800 per week. Off Broadway in NYC is usually around $500 or less per week.
Music Curation	Overseeing library or museum's music collection and presenting it. Not entirely unrelated to music librarianship.	Anywhere that has a historic collection of music that needs a curatorial manager. Libraries and museums are the most likely places, but some music colleges employ as well.	$50,000+

Music Education Administration	Works in administration of a public or private music education program, either at the K-12 or college level.	College music programs, high school music programs, private music lesson schools.	If below the Dean, between $20,000 and $60,000. If the Dean, over $100,000+.
Music Education Teacher (K-12)	Teaches at a public or private elementary, middle, or high school. Requires state certification and usually a Bachelor's in Music Education.	Pre-college educational institution.	Widely varies, but average starting salary is $30,000 – $40,000. Can be higher or lower based on the economic status of the institution.
Music/Entertainme nt Attorney	Attorney who represents artists as well as arts/entertainmen t organizations. Requires a JD (Juris Doctor degree) outside of a Bachelor's of Music degree.	In an entertainment law firm or as an independent attorney.	Varies widely. Working for a firm in a major city can provide starting salary of $150,000+.
Music Journalist/Critic	Someone who professionally reviews music performances, albums, and entertainment industry news.	Working for a media company (newspaper, magazine, online journal like *Pitchfork*) or having a blog yourself.	$25,000 – $150,000 (Careers In Music)
Music Librarian	A librarian specializing in cataloguing and maintaining music collections. Usually has a Bachelor's in Music and a Master's in either Music Librarianship or a Master of Library	Employment in a college, university, conservatory, orchestra, or public library.	$25,000 – $75,000 (Careers In Music)

	and Information Science.		
Music Supervisor	Someone who oversees all of the musical choices for a visual medium, including television, video games, advertisers, and films. Not to be confused with a commercial music composer.	Working on the staff of a television show or media company.	Annual salaries start at $30,000. Big-budget productions can hire music supervisors at $250,000 per project. (Wikipedia)
Musicologist	Someone who studies the history and culture of various musical genres. A research-based approach addressing scholarly inquiry of music.	As a lecturer or a professor in a university setting, and/or as a published author.	Typical salaries of a university professor (see Higher Education Teaching).
Music Therapist	Use music as a means of alternative therapy. Convincing evidence exists for treatment of depression and coronary heart disease.	Usually as independent worker with referrals from physicians, psychologists, physical therapists, and occupational therapists. Sometimes employed in higher education institutions, nursing homes, correctional facilities, and in intervention programs.	Around $50,000/yr (Musictherapy.org)

Online Music Teacher	Teach courses, either live or pre-recorded, using online video technology.	Almost always independently, although some businesses that stream specific music teachers' videos are emerging.	If live, recommended charge is between $40 – $100 per hour.
Opera Musician (Stage)	An artist who works either in a professional company or as a soloist performing operatic repertoire ranging from Mozart to Philip Glass.	Professional opera companies, freelance vocalist.	Varies widely; many professional opera companies can pay $30,000/yr, some higher-level ones can pay $60,000/yr, and the Metropolitan Opera can pay $200,000/yr.
Orchestral Musician	Musician who performs part-time or full-time as a member of an amateur or professional symphony orchestra.	Orchestras in the US, Canada, Europe, Asia, and South America are the best bets.	Depends on the orchestra, but here are some starting salaries for a variety of US orchestras:
Orchestral Musician	Musician who performs part-time or full-time as a member of an amateur or professional symphony orchestra.	Orchestras in the US, Canada, Europe, Asia, and South America are the best bets.	Chicago Symphony – $140,000 – $150,000
Orchestral Musician	Musician who performs part-time or full-time as a member of an amateur or professional symphony orchestra.	Orchestras in the US, Canada, Europe, Asia, and South America are the best bets.	Los Angeles Philharmonic – $140,000 – $150,000

Orchestral Musician	Musician who performs part-time or full-time as a member of an amateur or professional symphony orchestra.	Orchestras in the US, Canada, Europe, Asia, and South America are the best bets.	Philadelphia Orchestra – $100,000 –$110,000
Orchestral Musician	Musician who performs part-time or full-time as a member of an amateur or professional symphony orchestra.	Orchestras in the US, Canada, Europe, Asia, and South America are the best bets.	Dallas Symphony – $90,000 – $100,000
Orchestral Musician	Musician who performs part-time or full-time as a member of an amateur or professional symphony orchestra.	Orchestras in the US, Canada, Europe, Asia, and South America are the best bets.	San Diego Symphony – $55,000 – $65,000
Orchestral Musician	Musician who performs part-time or full-time as a member of an amateur or professional symphony orchestra.	Orchestras in the US, Canada, Europe, Asia, and South America are the best bets.	Alabama Symphony – $35,000 – $45,000
Orchestral Musician	Musician who performs part-time or full-time as a member of an amateur or professional symphony orchestra.	Orchestras in the US, Canada, Europe, Asia, and South America are the best bets.	Opera Cleveland (now out of business) – $151 per performance, about $40/hr for rehearsal

Orchestrator	Arranges a reduced score into a much larger score for an orchestra or larger ensemble.	Working for Broadway composers (then known as a Broadway Show Arranger), on the staff of film composers, or independently.	Professional, high-level orchestrators frequently charge $25 – $75 per 4 measures of orchestrated music. So, orchestrating an 80-measure composition could garner as much as a $1,500 payment. If orchestrating an entire Broadway score, that could equate to about 600 pages. With four fully orchestrated bars per page at an absolute minimum, orchestrating one show could pay, at $55 per 4 measures, over $30,000.
Piano Tuner	Creating adjustments to the strings of the piano so that its musical intervals are aligned properly, making it sound "in tune."	Independently or employed in a place where there is a need for piano tuners on site, like a music school.	$150 per tuning, or around $50,000+ annually if employed full-time
Pit Musician	A musician who plays in a musical, opera, or other live event.	Musicals, operas, and live events.	Up to $1,600. Requires membership in Musicians' Union (Berklee Salary Guide).
Private Music Teacher	Teaches students independently or in a school.	Independently or in school.	Between $30 – $120/hr
Publicist (music)	A person who creates buzz via publicity for a musician, band, music institution, business, etc.	Independently or with publicity firm.	Median is $55,000 (Education Portal)
Publisher Sales Representative (Informally, "Song Plugger")	An agent from a publishing company who sells compositions to labels and	Working for a publishing company.	$25,000 – $65,000

	artists for recording.		
Radio DJ	Acts as the public voice of the station, promotes a specific image to the audience.	Radio Stations.	Varies widely. Typical would be around $40,000 – $60,000
Record Producer	Oversees all aspects of an artist's album.	Working independently with an artist or with a record label.	Ranges widely depending on the producer and the projects he takes on, between 5 and 7 figures
Session Musician	Musician who plays on recording projects for different artists, labels, etc.	Working freelance on commercial recording projects.	Varies widely per musician, but can get into the six digits for the highest-paid professionals
Social Media Strategist	A savvy marketer who works with a company to promote their content online.	As a consultant or employed by a music company	$40,000 – $60,000. Other positions can bring in an income of six digits.
Sound / Acoustic Engineer	The application of sound and its composite elements, including frequencies and timbres, and applying it to specific technology. This can range anywhere from creating synthesizers to designing acoustically excellent concert halls.	Working for a company dealing with bioacoustics, audio signal processing, musical acoustics, noise control headphones, ultrasonic sound, etc.	Lucrative profession ranging from $70,000 – $150,000+

Sound Recordist	Someone who records sound and music using professional-level equipment, either in a studio or in a live performance setting.	Usually as an independent contractor	$35 – $100+ per hour
Stage Management	Organizing music, theater, dance, or multimedia production. Involves coordinating stage personnel, production managers, and more.	Working for a theater, dance company, or other arts organization.	Median is approximately $40,000 (Pay Scale)
Tour Director	Person responsible for coordinating all aspects of an artist's tour, including managing the road personnel, working in conjunction with an artist's publicist, etc.	Working personally with a band or with an artist management company.	The salary average is around $100,000.
Video Game Composer	Composer for the soundtrack and background of video games.	As an independent commercial music composer writing background music for video games.	Most video game composers make $1,000 – $2,000 per minute of music written. Smaller-budget games are usually $300 – $600.

Website Copywriter	Writes intelligent and informed biographies of different artists on a website for a performing arts company, record label, or other music business.	Writing online copy for a music company.	Median salary for copy editors in general is approximately $58,000 (Salary.com)
Website Designer	This is a space with a great deal of serving musicians and businesses.	Designing websites for musicians, usually as an independent contractor. Some website designers are employed in high-end design firms.	$20,000 – $200,000 +

As mentioned earlier, the United States Department of Labor Quick Facts appear in greater detail in Table 2.

Combined with the information listed in Table 1, you can develop a great knowledge of careers that appeal to your interests.

Most importantly, and armed with the statistics below, you will have a greater understanding of the economic outlook for each career type from the viewpoint of salary, education, experience level, and training level. You will also be able to understand the number of jobs filled in this category along with the outlook from a growth perspective.

TABLE 2.

Quick Facts	2016 Median Pay	Typical Entry-Level Education	Work Experience in a Related Occupation	On-the-job Training	Number of Jobs, 2016	Job Outlook, 2016-26	Employment Change, 2016-26
Advertising, Promotions, and Marketing Managers	$127,560 per year / $61.33 per hour	Bachelor's degree	None	None	249,600	10% (Faster than average)	23,800
Announcers	$30,830 per year / $14.82 per hour	Bachelor's degree	None	None	52,700	-9% (Decline)	-4,500
App Developers	$79,840 per year / $38.39 per hour	Bachelor's degree	None	None	294,900	-7% (Decline)	-21,300
Broadcast and Sound Engineering Technicians	$42,550 per year / $20.46 per hour	Bachelor's degree	None	None	134,300	8% (As fast as average)	10,700
Electrical and Electronics Engineering Technicians	$62,190 per year / $29.90 per hour	Associate's degree	None	None	137,000	2% (Slower than average)	2,700
Electrical and Electronics Engineers	$96,270 per year / $46.28 per hour	Bachelor's degree	None	None	324,600	7% (As fast as average)	21,300
Film and Video Editors and Camera Operators	$59,040 per year / $28.39 per hour	Bachelor's degree	None	None	59,300	13% (Faster than average)	7,600
High School Teachers	$58,030 per year	Bachelor's degree	None	None	1,018,700	8% (As fast as average)	76,800
Kinder-garten and Elementary	$55,490 per year	Bachelor's degree	None	None	1,565,300	7% (As fast as	116,300

School Teachers						averag e)	
Lawyers	$118,160 per year / $56.81 per hour	Doctoral or professio nal degree	None	None	792,50 0	8% (As fast as averag e)	65,000
Librarians	$57,680 per year / $27.73 per hour	Master's degree	None	None	138,20 0	9% (As fast as averag e)	12,400
Multimedia Artists	$65,300 per year / $31.40 per hour	Bachelor' s degree	None	None	73,700	8% (As fast as averag e)	6,200
Music Directors and Composers	$50,110 per year/$24 .09 per hour	Bachelor' s degree	Less than 5 years	None	74,800	6% (As fast as averag e)	4,300
Music Retail Sales	$22,900 per year / $11.01 per hour	No formal educatio nal credentia l	None	Yes	4,854,3 00	2% (Slowe r than averag e)	92,400
Music Sales Managers	$117,960 per year / $56.71 per hour	Bachelor' s degree	Less than 5 years	None	385,50 0	7% (As fast as averag e)	28,900
Photograph ers	$34,070 per year / $16.38 per hour	High school diploma or equivale nt	None	Long-term on-the-job trainin g	147,30 0	-6% (Decli ne)	-8,300
Post-secondary Teachers	$75,430 per year	Master's degree	None	None	1,314,4 00	15% (Much faster than averag e)	197,80 0
Producers and Directors	$70,950 per year / $34.11 per hour	Bachelor' s degree	Less than 5 years	None	134,70 0	12% (Faster than averag e)	16,500

63

Musicians and Singers	$25.14 per hour	No formal educatio nal credentia l	None	Long-term on-the-job trainin g	172,40 0	6% (As fast as averag e)	10,400
Recreational Therapists	$46,410 per year / $22.31 per hour	Bachelor' s degree	None	None	19,200	7% (As fast as averag e)	1,300
Reporters, Correspond ents, and Broadcast News Analysts	$38,870 per year / $18.69 per hour	Bachelor' s degree	None	None	50,400	-9% (Decli ne)	-4,500
Software Developers	$102,280 per year / $49.17 per hour	Bachelor' s degree	None	None	1,256,2 00	24% (Much faster than averag e)	302,50 0
Writers and Authors	$61,240 per year / $29.44 per hour	Bachelor' s degree	None	Long-term on-the-job trainin g	131,200	8% (As fast as averag e)	10,000

After reviewing and then defining the careers, statistics, and opportunities that match your interests and abilities, it will be time to conduct some additional research and figure out how best to launch your career.

Make sure you spend adequate time reviewing the information presented in Step #1 (inside this chapter).

Don't just skip Tables 1 and 2!

It's important to have a clear understanding of your goals and— from a career standpoint—where you would like to end up.

Step #2 — Research The Opportunities

By now—and certainly before you begin this next step—you should have a good idea of your goals, objectives, and what type of career you want to obtain in the music and/or entertainment industries.

Put more simply: You should now know what you **want to do**—and most importantly—what you **don't want to do.**

So—what's next?

Now is the time to research your opportunity down to *specific job offers*. In order to do this, you are going to return to a simple task used by virtually every newspaper and magazine writer.

The 5 Ws

You remember the 5 Ws from grade school, right? When writing a book report, your grade was based on whether or not you identified each of the following: "Who," "What," "Where," "When," "Why" (and sometimes "How").

You'll start by answering questions and then finish your research by applying the same fact-finding effort to ferret out the best careers available to you. Specifically:

- *Who* do you need to speak with to obtain a job?
- *What* are the exact job requirements, and *what* is the job description?
- *Where* are these careers located in relation to where you live?

66

- *When* is the best time to apply for a job?
- *Why* are they employing (or perhaps, why are they not employing)?
- *How* can you get the job today?

External Versus Internal Answers

Before you begin to answer the 5 Ws, which are *external* questions, we need to determine the answers to *internal* questions related to what makes you tick!

Specifically, you must obtain the answers to the following questions:

- *How* much time, money, and effort will it take for you to find your dream job?
- From an educational standpoint—*what* skills, knowledge, certification, degree do you need to properly function in the career you've identified? (In the previous section, see Table #2 columns #3 and #4 for this information.)
- *What* if you don't have the degree, certification, knowledge—is this something that you *can* acquire? *What* are the related time and investment expenses necessary to obtain the knowledge, certification, or degree?
- Does your return on the educational investment exceed the effort you have to spend? If not, *why* not?
- Does the institution (physical college/university versus an online operation) automatically provide you with job leads and placements? If so, *what* is their success rate?
- Does the educational institution provide you with referrals, that is, *actual employed graduates of their program*—that you

can speak to and undeniably determine that they are working in bona fide jobs in the music and entertainment industries?

- Can the educational institution guarantee that the majority of their graduates or certified students are actually working?
- *What* job placement, career advancement, and after-graduation/certification services are available to you?

It's important to create and catalog your questions and answers for each job or career type you're interested in. In the next section of the book (Step #3), I will show you how to find the answers to these questions. For this section, though, it is just important that you put these questions together.

Company-Specific Questions:

Now that you have most of the *internal* questions ready to be researched, we need to look *externally,* using a different set of criteria than the 5 Ws. This is where you ask questions directly to the companies you're seeking employment from.

At this stage, it's important not to limit your questions and research to a single job type. You must search all the careers related to the companies you're considering. For example:

- *Which* company or organization represents the right opportunities by offering the exact or closest match to what you want to achieve in your career?
- *What* place of work has the most positive and accepting work culture?

- *Which* company has the location that is either closest to where you currently live or provides an opportunity to live in another city?
- *What* specific industry contributions does this organization make?

If the company you research misses the mark on certain answers above, do not despair. Rarely is a new job or career opportunity an A+ in all categories and characteristics.

Should you find yourself with research leading to less than the perfect ideal career or job opportunities, take a deep breath.

Could this still be a launching pad for you to start your career by getting your foot in the door and then advancing to a better position that's more in line with your ultimate dream job?

You'd better believe it could. Go back and review my history for proof!

Remember that even if your initial career move or organization isn't perfect, you can always leverage your experience and the cachet of a company brand in your next career opportunity.

Remember this: Your first job in the music and entertainment industries does not necessarily have to be your last job.

Step #3 — Conduct Your Research

By now—and having completed Steps #1 and #2—you should have an excellent collection of notes. Included in these are one or more specific **goals** that point you to the career that most interests you.

You should also have **statistical and descriptive information** about these jobs, their salaries, the market buoyancy, how many career opportunities exist, and what the 10-year outlook is.

Not just that, but you should have a substantial list of **research questions** related to each job. This includes research addressing the 5 Ws, questions about how much of an investment you need to make along with the return you can expect for each job, and specific company and organizational questions to help you to find the perfect (or most optimal) fit for your next first career move.

Armed with both a game plan (your goal) and research (your questions related to this goal), you are now poised to acquire the answers and chart your path to success.

Research Defined

Remember that **research** is defined as a "careful and diligent search." While collecting information, the act of researching also includes three important facts:

1. Investigations aimed at the **discovery of facts**;
2. **Revising presumptions** in the light of these new facts; and
3. **Practical application** of answered, new, or revised facts.

You'll note the repetition of the word "facts."

This is because—in spite of your excitement and emotional desire to be employed in the music and/or entertainment industry—you need to divorce yourself from such passion, instincts, *and* feelings.

Instead, and throughout this Step #3...your sole focus should be on—you guessed it—**Just The Facts**.

Where To Start Researching

Most of your competition (and most people, regardless of the industry they are interested in) start researching by checking out employment ads or using online career search engines.

While there is nothing inherently wrong with these tools, please know that you will be competing with a larger number of job applicants because so many people start their career search this way.

I would, however, respectfully and humbly suggest ___you___ ___look elsewhere.___

Specifically, you are in search of secret, inside information about job openings and career opportunities that fewer numbers of people are aware of.

Why?

Your odds of acquiring these types of jobs and careers increases dramatically, particularly when fewer people are competing for the same positions.

Read the sentence above again—three more three times. It is critical that you understand this. Here's a real-life example of why this is so important.

In my own career search, I was the only candidate for the first three jobs I obtained. They were filled immediately by me because I was the only person who knew about the jobs. I carefully and exhaustively researched these companies, and no one else even knew that these jobs were available.

By networking my way to each job offering, I was able to interview for the positions before the markets were advised of the job openings. Better still, I received and accepted three job offers before any other candidates were even considered for interviews. In fact—and in two of the three positions—I received the job offers even before my predecessors knew they were about to be let go.

To repeat, the important part of finding jobs and careers that only a few people know about will be critical to your success...both in your first and subsequent jobs.

How to Conduct Research Secretively
Given this, how do you obtain information about job opportunities and answer your research questions from Step #2 that match up with your goals from Step #1.

- Do you require friends in high places?
- Do you need to be a spy?
- Do you need a British accent?
- Do you have to change your last name to "Bond"?

Thankfully, you don't need any of these things. You do need to exercise some effort to sleuth out very special opportunities.

Wait...You Want Me to Start Online?

Yes, you *should* start your research ONLINE, using many of the venerable career-building websites. In doing so, you will acquire a "lay of the land" that reveals what jobs are available **to the masses**.

By all means, if any of these jobs are interesting to you, make a note.

More often than not, however, you'll likely not apply to these positions.

Why?

These jobs should be avoided because the odds of gainful employment are statistically stacked against you. This is due to the large number of inquiries and size of the population reading and responding to these openings.

Let me reiterate—I would strongly suggest that online listings are NOT necessarily going to be the precise jobs for you. You're looking for a "diamond career job opening."

And finding a diamond in a haystack of online listings isn't going to be as easy when researching *monster.com, indeed.com,* or *ziprecruiter.com.*

You're going to need to move **offline**.

This means meeting with **people**.

Yup. **Face-to-face.**

People—and not computers.

Because, in the end, it will be a person who hires you.

Not a computer.

Chuck the Internet, Focus on the Chamber, Yield to the Yellow Pages

So, where do you go to meet influential people who hold the keys to your career?

To begin with, and depending on what city you currently live in, I would suggest starting by contacting the local chamber of commerce and using the Yellow Pages (yellowpages.com if you prefer).

Begin by making telephone calls and find out what businesses offer the jobs you're most interested in. If, for example, you're interested in app developers for audio engineering professionals, find out what companies create these products by reaching out to the local chamber of commerce or by "letting your fingers do the walking" while searching the Yellow Pages.

On the other hand, if you're interested in working for an advertising agency having an in-house audio studio that creates background music, voice-overs, and related sound deliverables, contact the Chamber or review the Yellow Pages to determine which organizations fill these types of jobs.

If the location you are interested yields companies that fit your research questions and goals, then you are ready for the next step. If not, you may need to look into different cities and broaden your search.

Pay People a Visit

Armed with real businesses' addresses and telephone numbers—it will be time to have *informational interviews*. These are informal meetings with chamber of commerce administrators and members along with potential companies that might be hiring. The goal is as follows:

1. You contact a real person.
2. You schedule telephone conversations, in-person meetings, or even coffee for a short encounter, and
3. You research the answers to your questions.

By having an informal chat with someone at the business level (whether it is someone at your local Chamber's business development department—or perhaps with someone in the human resources department of a company you actually want to work with), you can determine who is hiring, who is growing, and who isn't.

If a chamber employee provides you with information about a company that you're interested in, by all means: Call that organization and mention the name of the chamber person who referred you. And when you do speak with someone at the business you want to work for, ask if they are hiring.

Most importantly—and whether at the chamber or company level—get to know people, and let them get to know you.

Don't Stop Until You Get Enough

In addition to meeting face-to-face with chambers and local businesses, I strongly urge you to meet and research local, regional, and national music and entertainment *organizations*. These groups typically cater to practicing professionals in job and career categories that you've targeted.

This "organizational" hint applies not only to professional groups but also to local unions and lead generation groups. Both meet regularly for social and networking opportunities. Many of these meetings are listed in local, free newspapers and magazines, as well as online sources like MeetUp.com.

It's important to attend these events because you are likely to meet professionals connected with your field of interest. They are also likely to know of specific job opportunities.

When meeting with these members, be certain to schedule informational interviews when following up. You should also meet with group leaders, administrators, officers, and board members.

Basically, focus on learning from *anyone* who has their finger on the pulse of your target job market. Don't be surprised if these individuals hold full-time positions at the companies where you want to work.

In the end, the more people you consistently come in contact with (i.e., networking), the more likely you will be able to develop personal relationships. From these relationships comes knowledge of those hidden, diamond jobs that (hopefully) only you'll know about.

Checklist

Here are a few items to consider when conducting your research. To begin, acquire a lay-of-the-land understanding of popular job offerings by reviewing:

- Indeed.com
- Monster.com
- CareerBuilder.com
- LinkedIn.com
- ZipRecruiter.com

Don't forget to search offline by looking up information:

- When speaking with local businesses in the area
- Using the Yellow Pages
- With growing companies/members in your chamber of commerce
- At the local musician's union—the American Federation of Musicians
- With local/national chapters of the Audio Engineering Society and other local professional groups
- Through local chapters of the National Association of Broadcasters and/or the Society of Motion Picture and Television Engineers
- With traditional advertising and digital marketing agencies who perform audio/music tasks

Attend Conventions, Conferences, Expositions, and Exhibitions
One of the best ways to connect with the largest collection of companies allied to the music and entertainment industry is to attend national, regional, and international conventions. These events (which are sometimes called conferences, expositions, and exhibitions) include:

- The National Association of Broadcasters
- The Audio Engineering Society
- The Society of Motion Picture and Television Engineers
- The Consumer Electronic Show
- National Association of Music Merchants
- Game Developers Conference
- InfoComm
- Electronic Entertainment Expo
- Penny Arcade Expo
- GenCon

When attending these events, be certain to spend time on the floor perusing products and services as well as meeting decision-makers face-to-face. You will also want to visit round-table discussions, white papers, and new technology presentations.

At these conferences, make a special point of meeting guest speakers. More importantly, focus on meeting the **conference moderators.** It's usually the moderators who are equally, if not more, connected to a large network of jobs that you want to learn about. Also, event moderators are less likely be swamped prior to and following presentations.

Don't forget these other great networking opportunities:

- There will likely be plenty of free corporate and group parties. Be sharp. Don't party *too* hard. Listen and learn.
- Don't forget to search job boards at the convention communication centers.
- When meeting with companies, think beyond networking to their human resources. Aim to connect to your target organization's design, service, technical, and sales and marketing executives.

Navigate Your Own Network

Don't forget about your own network of contacts that you have cultivated over the years. Many people you already know may have moved into positions at companies and are either hiring or can help point you in the right direction.

For these reasons, keep in touch with:

- Old classmates, friends, and professors
- Other educators and instructors from your trade school, college, or university
- Certification attendees and instructors
- Administrators from previous organizations, schools, and facilities
- Administrators and executives at job placement offices, career shows, and job fairs
- Mentors and professional coaches

Step #4 — Create Deliverables

Up to this point, if you've attended to Steps #1, #2, and #3, you have accomplished a tremendous amount. By now, you should feel very proud about having:

1. Defined your **goal** and identified the **job** you want in the music or entertainment industry.
2. **Researched** the opportunities about specific jobs, their description, salaries, growth opportunities, and overall industry climate; and
3. Conducted your search to identify specific jobs and **employers** and have met with people in a position to recommend or hire you.

You might imagine that you are now ready to make appointments with prospective employers and start interviewing for available positions. In truth, while you are *able* to do this, I would *strongly advise against it*.

Why?

There is still work to be done in preparing for a successful interview.

Rather than making appointments, take a deep breath.

I am going to suggest that you take two more giant steps forward in order to *differentiate* yourself from other job candidates who may have conducted research similar to yours. You want to be certain that you adequately distinguish yourself from others so that employers will notice you first. You want to position yourself to be *the best*—if not *only*—candidate for the job.

One of two ways to accomplish this is listed here in Step #4. You are going to create **deliverables**: a thing able to be provided, especially prior to and during your interview.

Nowadays, it is no longer sufficient to provide a resume (a type of deliverable) when seeking or meeting someone at your interview.

In particular—and because you're seeking employment in any number of creative jobs—you will require more than a piece of paper to differentiate yourself from others.

And no—a portfolio of your recordings, lyrics, and a website—is not enough.

Although these will not hurt to have in your arsenal, they shouldn't be the focal point. Like the resume, they should represent a portion of those items you make available to obtain and present during your interview.

What I am talking about is something *considerably more targeted*. Something that is meaningful to the prospective employer and their company.

Deliverables that show you are not just *any ordinary applicant*.

Deliverables that reveal *you are the perfect and, if possible, only candidate for the job*.

Sound good?

Of course it does.

The Perfect Deliverable

The perfect item to present is the one that is:

- *Relevant* to the job description you're attempting to fill.
- Meaningful to the organization and *makes a contribution* to them.
- Uniquely relates to your abilities.

Let me give you an example that enabled me to get my foot in the door for an interview during my third year at the university. This example cemented the offer I received within days of my interview.

After transferring to my second college, it was suggested—because of my love of writing—that I create product reviews for a notable industry publication: *Mix Magazine*. (*Mix* is still available today and is considered the leading record studio and live sound publication for the music industry).

The editor assigned me a highly technical article...something I wasn't terribly expert at. I'm not referring to equipment operation, which I was very skilled at. I'm talking about connecting equipment to test benches in order to perform specific scientific measurements. These metrics are necessary to determine the accuracy of a manufacturer's claims.

Think of my writing job as a *Consumer Reports* for high-end audio equipment.

With considerable assistance from my professors, I tore the equipment apart, down to its components, and documented the specific performance issues.

From there, I authored a very tight 1,500-word article, complete with product photographs, diagrams, and specifications. In the end, I finished my first published article (e.g., a cool first **deliverable** for job interviews).

And while I hadn't scheduled my first job interview before it was published, I was paid ten cents a word for the article. For a college kid, the $150 payday came in handy when running to the University Rathskeller for a few beers following the weekly football game!

Most importantly, my first article—about a high-powered studio loudspeaker amplifier—led to my second article.

And the second article was pivotal in obtaining my first real job in the industry.

Why?

The second piece of equipment I reviewed was a very large format (32+ channel) recording studio mixing console. This was one from a well-known British manufacturer that you might find in a recording studio's B-Room.

Funnily enough, I was living at my parents' home while attending the university when—one afternoon—a large 18-wheeler tractor-trailer pulled up to our front door. Three large men who asked for me removed three gigantic crates from their vehicle.

Fortunately, I happened to be home to accept the delivery and calm my parents down. This thing was a beast.

Over the course of the next month, I lugged this console around town and put it through its paces. With the help of friends who had large flat-bed trucks and vans at their disposal, I brought the equipment to our university studios and plugged into our laboratory test bench. I delved into every aspect of this console and fell in love with it.

The article that ensued was a joy to write. I certainly had a better—though not comprehensive—knowledge of how to test equipment specifications (thank to my professors and my prior amplifier experience).

While the second paycheck was expected and welcomed, what occurred within a month of the article's publication was completely unexpected.

Professor Ken Pohlmann called me into his office one afternoon, describing a telephone call he'd received from the president/owner of a competing console manufacturing company located in Chicago. Apparently, the owner read the article, which positioned his competitor in a very favorable light. Needless to say, this "angered" him a bit as he wanted *his* console to be reviewed...not his competitor's.

He called my professor (my editor), wanting to know who had written the article. As it turns out, the owner's anger would better be described as jealousy. More to the point, the owner wanted to learn more about me and my availability to replace his soon-to-be-leaving vice president of sales.

During my Chicago interview, which occurred the week that followed the aforementioned telephone call, the owner referred to the article during every introduction he made when I met each of his employees. They were mystified that a "college kid" had upset the apple cart so much. Apparently, everyone was amused that I somehow "got under the boss's skin" and, as a result, "I was going to be hired."

Honestly, I was rather naive and did not buy into the drama. I had just taken a flight to Chicago, spent the day at a cool manufacturing plant, and returned home to find a letter offering employment that weekend.

The point is this: It wasn't my resume, audio recordings, school transcript, or any *typical* piece of paper that I might have sent to secure a job interview.

Far from it; it was a <u>considerably tailored deliverable</u> that did the trick.

Remember, it was *a deliverable that had meaning to the employer.*

It paved the way for the interview, figured prominently during my interview, and resulted in the nearly immediate contract of employment that followed.

This deliverable not only touched a nerve, but it proved to be the ideal "calling card" and entré for my first job as a professional in the music industry.

Maybe writing equipment review isn't your specialty. You might be more of a technical or scientific person who feels more comfortable researching and authoring "white papers." Or maybe you want to present a technical article that might be heralded at a local organization or trade show.

Still not your cup of tea? No problem—how about these deliverables:

- Album or music reviews for both online and printed periodicals
- Local music scene newsletters covering live performances
- Blog or V-log for specific genres, instruments, practice techniques, and educational strategies
- YouTube channels for entertainment-specific issues

All of these are ideal, provided that they significantly connect to your skill-sets, career goals, and employer you want to interview with.

Remember: If there's not a meaningful link (as was the case with my magazine articles), then search for another deliverable.

But Wait — There's More!

Of course, there are other interview deliverables you should have at your fingertips. These are more perfunctory in nature and include your:

- Personal **website** (which can be a placeholder for all of your other deliverables along with links to them).
- **LinkedIn** page with up-to-date education, experience, and personal summary.
- Your **FaceBook** and online groups pages. Make sure your personal page posting is suitable for work. If it isn't, clean it up today.

The bottom line is this...

The more deliverables you can create that meaningfully connect to your career and prospective employer—the better. Any deliverable that makes a contribution to the organization and their customers is likely to get you the interview—and hopefully, the job of your choice.

So get to work. Start creating your deliverables today, and make sure they line up with the career you're interested in.

And don't forget to polish off that resume, too.

Step #5 — Create & Participate In Professional Groups

In Step #4, you learned one of two important "pre-interview" initiatives to tend to—the creation of "Deliverables."

In this step, you will now learn of the second maneuver that, like the deliverables, will differentiate you from other job applicants. This step involves networking in professional groups.

There are many professional groups—even for those unemployed in the music and entertainment industry—that will welcome your involvement, membership, and attendance. Participation not only enables you to gain access to inside information about job availability, but you'll also learn about:

- Industry practices and professional standards
- Professional development
- Cultural enrichment
- Education
- Human services programs
- Advocacy

And of course, many groups have their own awards and recognition programs that you can attend and participate in.

If you're in school, I recommend participating in professional groups that have educational or student memberships. Not only are dues considerably less expensive, but specific events are often created just for students and soon-to-be professionals.

And while there are organizations for nearly every interest in the music and entertainment industry, they may not exist where you live. If this happens to be the case, check your nearby community college or university system, and see if a section is located there.

If you still come up empty-handed, I recommend reaching out to the professional organization's main offices to inquire if you can start a group.

In fact, that is precisely what I did.

Although my alma mater—the University of Miami—was established in 1925, the School Of Music (established a year later) never instituted an Audio Engineering Society Student Section. This was pretty ironic, particularly since the School of Music was the *birthplace* of the nation's first music engineering program.

One of the hallmarks of the Music Engineering program is that it requires students to immerse themselves and master electrical and computer engineering courses—not just art/music classes.

Given all of this, it seemed a bit odd to me that the Audio Engineering Society wasn't affiliated with the university. I thought the professional group would be a "complementary fit" for the curriculum and its students.

With that thought, I contacted the AES headquarters in New York City. I identified myself as a sophomore at the university and expressed my desire to charter their first student chapter.

The administrators could not have been kinder to me. Not only were we immediately chartered as a student group, we were instructed on how to set up financial and administrative accounts. Thereafter, we were provided with funding for programming events. I recall that several thousand dollars were "gifted" to our group, and I was going to make good use of these funds.

Remembering that at the time, digital audio was in its nascent years, I wanted to make a big splash with our inaugural student chapter event. With the help of my mentor, Professor Ken Pohlmann, I invited one of digital audio's pioneers—the legendary Dr. Roger Lagadec from Studer/ Revox in Regensdorf, Switzerland—to meet his new Miami fan base.

Dr. Lagadec was instrumental in co-authoring multiple patents related to recording, reproducing, and editing the transmission of digitized signals and sound on audio equipment. When you think of digital recording devices like tape, compact disc, computers, or portable tablets and mobile phones—you should think of—*and thank*—Dr. Lagadec.

As the inaugural president and founding member of the University of Miami's Audio Engineering Society, I wanted to bring Dr. Lagadec to the United States to speak to our emerging group of student audio engineers.

This was an incredibly humbling and educational experience. Remember, this was at a time when the internet was not prevalent (let alone available for searching and securing air, hotel, and ground travel). Logistically speaking, it was a challenge—and without email—to communicate with Dr. Lagadec.

In addition to hosting Dr. Lagadec for his University of Miami debut, I was able to carve out meaningful social time with him away from the university. Thanks to my Uncle Stuart Grossman, we spent Dr. Lagadec's post-speaking engagement time enjoying each other's company. Over the weekend, and along with my professors, we boated, dined, and relaxed in the Florida Keys.

My work with the University of Miami's AES chapter enabled me to travel to some of the greatest trade shows and conferences in the world's busiest cities. Membership afforded me the opportunity to meet with great industry leaders; moreover, it kick-started my career in professional audio design and sales and marketing.

Clearly, I am a huge proponent of participating in professional groups. I highly recommend you do so starting early in your career. If possible, don't just be a passive member; get involved, give back, and reap the rewards that only active participation offers.

Student-Run Organizations

The following table provides a great starting point for organizations related to the music and entertainment industries. While not exhaustive in scope, the list should be incorporated as a starting point in your employment strategy.

Organization	Description
AES (Audio Engineering Society)	Promotes research and commercial interests of designers, manufacturers, buyers, and users of professional and semiprofessional audio equipment.
AFM (American Federation of Musicians)	Assists musicians in the US and Canada with fair agreements, music ownership, and benefits.
AIMP (Association of Independent Music Publishers)	Educates music publishers about the most current industry trends by providing a forum for discussing the issues confronting the publishing industry.
AMP (Association of Music Producers)	Educates its members as well as the production, advertising, and media communities on all facets of music production, from creation to final use.
AMTA (American Music Therapy Association)	Organization for the progressive development of the therapeutic use of music in rehabilitation, special education, and community settings.
AMTAS (American Music Therapy Association for Students)	Promotes awareness, use, and development of music therapy in order to maximize health.
APAP (Association of Performing Arts Presenters)	World's largest networking forum and marketplace for performing arts professionals including artists, agents, and emerging leaders.
ASCAP (American Society of Composers, Authors and Publishers)	Performing rights organization representing over 420,000 songwriters, composers, and music publishers.
BMI (Broadcast Music, Inc.)	Performing rights organization that collects license fees on behalf of songwriters, composers, and music

	publishers and distributes them as royalties to members.
ISME (International Society for Music Education)	Serves music educators around the world; represents all levels and all fields of specialization within music education.
ISPA (International Society for the Performing Arts)	Develops and educates an international network of leaders and professionals who are dedicated to advancing the performing arts.
MIDEM (Marché International du Disque et de l'Edition Musicale)	World's largest music industry trade fair providing a forum for discussing political and legal issues, new artists, musical trends, and music-related products.
MTNA (Music Teachers National Association)	Cultivates growth and development for music teaching professionals.
Music Business Association	Nonprofit trade association that seeks to advance and promote music commerce, whether physical, digital, mobile, or more.
NAFME (National Association for Music Education)	Connection between music educators, national conferences, and the industry.
NAMM (National Association of Music Merchants)	Strengthens the music products industry and promotes the benefits of making music.
NARIP (National Association of Record Industry Professionals)	Creates access to top executives and experts in the music and record industries.
RIAA (Recording Industry Association of America)	North and South American trade organization that represents the recording industry in the United States.

SESAC (Society of European Stage Authors and Composers)	Performing rights organization in the US with a selective process when affiliating songwriters and publishers.
SPARS (Society of Professional Audio Recording Studios)	Unites the manufacturers of audio recording equipment and services with users.
The GRAMMY Awards (The Recording Academy)	Honors achievements in the recording arts and supports the music community.
WFMT (World Federation of Music Therapy)	International non-profit organization that brings together music therapy associations and individuals interested in developing and promoting music therapy globally.

Step #6 — Interview

Now...yes, now...you are finally ready to interview for your job/career.

You are not just halfway through this checklist, you are on the precipice of being able to conquer your goal and become gainfully employed in the music or entertainment industries.

Why?

Because you've clearly **defined** your objective, **researched** your opportunities, **conducted** your search, **created** deliverables, and **participated** in professional groups.

You are now ready to set up appointments and begin the interview process.

Before you head out on your first—of which may be many—interviews, I strongly suggest considering all the tips listed in this sub-chapter. To begin with, here are the:

Top 5 Interviewing Tips Specifically for the Music and Entertainment Industries.

- <u>Tip #1</u>—Analyze the specific music or entertainment job you're interested in—not just the career, or the industry, or the organization. You want to know *the exact daily job requirements*.

- Tip #2—How does the specific job match with your *skill-sets and abilities*? Create a list, and be aware of mentioning your capabilities during your interview.

- Tip #3—Be *honest*. Because you can't possibly know everything, you have to be willing to learn *more*. Show humility, be authentic, and provide examples of how you've learned quickly and comprehensively in the past. Be certain to mention how learning was of benefit to others—especially if learning was on-the-job while employed elsewhere.

- Tip #4—*Research* the company where you are interviewing. Don't just analyze what they make, service, or provide. Determine exactly how they compare to others in their industry. Identify their customers' opinions. You may be able to contribute to the company and help correct what isn't so good, or sustain what is working.

- Tip #5—*Practice* interviewing. Set up a place and time for a mock interview process. You want to be comfortable and confident when attending real interviews. Consider rehearsing with friends or family members for both in-person, telephone, and online interviews. Create a list of questions, and be able to answer by practicing your responses in front of others. Don't just do this by yourself.

The "Dreaded Question"

What should you do if you're asked the dreaded question: "Why are you leaving your current job?"

A good, safe, and common answer is to reply along the lines of your desire to continue challenging yourself, and in the role that you're in now, you've gone as far as you can.

You can mention that you would like to push yourself further, to learn more, to challenge yourself further, and improve your skills while helping a team succeed.

Don't forget to confirm your understanding of the role you're interviewing for and the attributes of the company you're interviewing with. Mention exactly why these both interest and excite you.

Although this may not have been specifically asked of you, it was implied in the "Dreaded Question." By mentioning your understanding of the job role, etc., you will reiterate your positivity and your interest in the position.

Accentuate the Positive

As a final note, interviewers may push you beyond the "Dreaded Question." Because the door has been opened with respect to your current/former employer, interviewers may probe further, asking you questions about what your company is doing right or wrong.

Whatever the answer might "truly" be, it is often best to keep your answers *positive*. Whether about your associates, your superiors, or your company, it is advisable to avoid saying anything *negative*.

There is a beautiful quotation attributable to both Abraham Lincoln and Mark Twain that applies here:

"Better to remain silent and be thought a fool than to speak and to remove all doubt."

Oftentimes, you will be tested in interviews to expose your foolishness. Remember that speaking negatively is one characteristic that is frowned on by job interviewers. Don't be fooled.

Differentiating Yourself During the Interview
In addition to using the Deliverables mentioned in Step #4, you can further substantiate why you are the best candidate by articulating the following personal characteristics during your interview:

- **<u>Under Pressure:</u>** Mention how you work well under pressure and how this was a benefit to other people, companies, and organizations. For example, during your school project, or perhaps while working part time in a studio, mention your experience with a band or artist that required you to create multiple mixes and edits of a singular track before the artist felt comfortable selecting the "correct" version. That you had to perform multiple mixes for all twelve tracks while setting a "land speed" world record was "all in a day's work" for you.

- **<u>Handling Challenges</u>**: Identify, describe, and catalog your successes. You might explain how you produced recordings of a touring band that took 2 days in the studio to record an entire album live. After the band left to return to the road, you were to edit and mix from the takes they'd recorded. You learned that the recording engineer accidentally combined the snare drum and left piano microphone onto one track. You were left to rectify the problem and keep the project on schedule and within budget. By reworking the tracks without having to bring the drummer and keyboardist back into town, you handled the challenge beautifully and were a hero to all.

- **Identify Unforced Errors**: We all make mistakes. Humbly and positively describe how you corrected an error that rested squarely on your shoulders. You might describe how—in the middle of a computer backup of your project—you lost 8 of the 15 tracks that were previously recorded and mixed. All archives, backups, and original files were completely damaged—unusable. Without batting an eye, you took it upon yourself to pay for and assume all responsibilities to correct the damage. The client, management, and all personnel involved were grateful to you. Your efforts resulted in you booking more business for the studio because you handled everything with humility and respect.

- **Goal-Setting**: Interviews offer a great opportunity to explain how you have set goals, modified your strategies to achieve goals, and what the outcome was. If you were in a sales position, you might mention what your original sales quotas were, how an increase caused you to develop new strategies, and what effect this had on the company's net profit.

- **Unpopular Decisions**: Describe how you made an unpopular decision and its outcome work for your previous company, its employees, and your customers. This will reveal your wisdom and capabilities to any potential employer.

- **Teamwork**: Indicating how you function as a team member is often critical in today's business environment. Revealing how you motivated, trained, and inspired your sales team to achieve a 350% profit increase would be coveted by any prospective employer.

- **Disagreements Dissolved**: Your ability to describe how you handled a disagreement with someone at work and its swift resolution is an ideal characteristic to mention during your interview. For example, your design department was not willing to listen to the marketing coordinator and take customer requests when creating a product update. After linking the customer directly with the design department, you "green-lighted" product enhancements, resulting in a sales increase of 375%!

- **Difficult Situations**: Handling a difficult situation can be a wonderful bonus to describe during your interview. By way of example, a new vice president of sales was hired to replace the outgoing employee. On her first day of work, the new VP arrived and was surprised to see the sales director (who previously reported to the former VP) sitting in her chair. He had errantly assumed that he was being promoted to the VP of sales. The actual and newly hired VP navigated this difficult situation by speaking directly to the company owner, garnering advice, and then gently—but firmly—correcting the sales director's loyalty and respect.

Sample Interview Questions

Armed with interviewing tips and ways you can differentiate yourself from the competition, I am happy to present a tremendous timesaver to you now.

I've collected over 100 sample interview questions that, if carefully reviewed and answered, will help you immensely.

In fact, if you print each question on a 3" x 5" index card and write down a thoughtful answer on the reverse, you will be 95% ahead of everyone else interviewing for the same position.

Better still, give these cards to a family member or friend, and rehearse your answers with them.

Seriously...do it right now. It's critical that you create the cards, and even more important that you *speak* the answers multiple times so that you are comfortable, confident, and comprehensive in your answers.

100+ Interview Questions

1. Tell me about yourself.
2. What are your greatest strengths?
3. What are your weaknesses?
4. How do you handle challenges and failures?
5. What about your successes?
6. Tell me something that's NOT on your resume.
7. How will your greatest strength help our company?
8. Do you consider yourself successful, and why?
9. How do you handle stress and pressure?

10. How would you describe yourself?

11. Are you an organized person?

12. What do you think a typical work week would be like?

13. Are you lucky?

14. Are you nice?

15. Are you willing to fail?

16. Can you describe your work style?

17. Do you work better with others or by yourself?

18. Do you take work home with you?

19. How are you different from others seeking this job?

20. How do you view yourself, and whom do you see as your competitors?

21. How does this job fit in with your career plan?

22. How many hours a week do you normally work?

23. How would you adjust to working for a new company?

24. What pace do you work at?

25. How would coworkers describe your personality?

26. What motivates you?

27. Are you self-motivated?

28. What are the most difficult decisions for you to make?

29. What's been the greatest disappointment of your life?

30. What are you passionate about?

31. What are your hobbies?

32. What annoys you?

33. What is your dream job?

34. What will you miss most about your last job?

35. What will you NOT miss about your last job?

36. Would you rather be liked or respected?

37. Why should our company take a risk on hiring you?

38. If you could live the last 10 years of your life differently, what would you do?

39. Why are you leaving your current/last job?

40. Why do you want to change jobs?

41. Why were you fired?

42. Why were you laid off?

43. Why did you quit your job?

44. Why did you resign?

45. What have you been doing since your last job?

46. Why have you been out of work so long?

47. What were your starting and final levels of compensation?

48. What are your salary expectations?

49. What are your salary requirements?

50. Why would you take a job for less money?

51. What applicable experience do you have?

52. Are you overqualified for this job?

53. How did you impact the bottom line?

54. Sell me this pen. Ready? Set? Go!

55. What can you do better for us versus other job candidates?

56. What part of the job will be the least challenging for you?

57. Which parts of this job are the most challenging?

58. What philosophy guides your work?

59. What strength will help you most to succeed?

60. Why are you interested in taking a lower-level job?

61. Why are you interested in a non-management job?

62. What do people most often criticize about you?

63. What is the biggest criticism you received from your boss?

64. What is the worst thing that you have ever gotten away with?

65. What makes you angry?

66. What problems have you encountered at work?

67. What strategies would you use to motivate your team?

68. What would you be looking for in an applicant?

69. When was the last time you were angry at work, and what happened?

70. Why weren't you promoted at your last job?

71. Tell me something you would have done differently at work.

72. If people who know you were asked why you should be hired, what would they say?

73. What type of work environment do you prefer?

74. How do you evaluate success?

75. Describe a difficult work situation or project and how you overcame it.

76. Describe a time when your workload was heavy and how you handled it.

77. Regarding your prior job, what were your expectations? Were they met?

78. What were your responsibilities?

79. What major challenges and problems did you face, and how did you handle them?

80. What have you learned from your mistakes?

81. What did you like or dislike about your previous job?

82. Which was most/least rewarding?

83. Were you ever demoted, and what was the reason/result?

84. How have you impacted worker safety?

85. Describe the gap in your employment history.

86. Who was your best boss, and who was the worst?

87. Describe your ideal boss.

88. If you were aware that your boss was 100% wrong about something, how would you handle it?

89. What do you expect from a supervisor?

90. Have you ever had difficulty working with a manager?

91. How did you fit in with the company culture?

92. Describe how you managed a problem employee.

93. Do you prefer to work independently or on a team?

94. Give examples of teamwork.

95. Why should we hire you?

96. Why shouldn't we hire you?

97. Why should we hire you instead of other job applicants?

98. Why are you the best person for the job?

99. What can you contribute to this company?

100. How is our company better than your current employer?

101. What interests you about this job?

102. What do you know about this company?

103. Why do you want this job?

104. Why do you want to work here?

105. What challenges are you looking for in a position?

106. What do you see yourself doing within the first 30 days on the job?

107. What can we expect from you in the first 60 days on the job?

108. Are you willing to travel?

109. How would you define good customer service?

110. What is your ideal company culture?

111. When could you start work?

112. Is there anything I haven't told you about the job or company that you would like to know?

113. What are you looking for in your next job, and what is important to you?
114. What is your professional development plan?
115. Where do you see yourself 5 years from now?
116. Where do you see yourself in 10 years?
117. What are your goals for the next 5 years/10 years?
118. How do you plan to achieve your goals?
119. What will you do if you don't get this position?
120. Where else are you interviewing?
121. Do you have any questions for me?

Remember: If you want to be fully prepared to acquire the career of your dreams, you should *review*, *speak*, and *role-play* your answers to all the questions above.

Don't just skim through them.

It's important that you practice verbalizing your thoughts and hearing yourself say the words when answering the questions above. If you like, video or audio record your role-playing and review/listen to your answers.

In doing so, you will have a greater sense of calm, comfort, and confidence during your actual interviews.

Step #7 — Follow Up & Negotiate Terms

In this day and age, few if any people write letters.

You know…the ones you create with paper, pen, and proper handwriting!

To make the best impression on those who might hire you for your next job, and to set yourself apart from every other applicant, I strongly suggest you contact the person(s) who interviewed you immediately after spending time with them.

Yes, I would immediately have an email ready for them.

Make certain to highlight one to three specific takeaways in your email. These should recapitulate the main reasons why you are the *correct* person for the job.

Be gracious, and don't forget to invite your contact to telephone or email you should they have any questions about your capabilities.

Then—for extra measure—write (yes…*write* with a pen, nice paper, and your best handwriting) a letter thanking your interviewer(s) for the opportunity to meet, speak, and learn from them. Again, highlight an *additional* reason why you can contribute to their organization and that you're available to continue the dialogue if they have any questions.

Most importantly, send your letter in a *United States Priority Mail Envelope* so it arrives quickly in a specially marked package. FedEx,

UPS, and other services are equally acceptable—but usually more expensive.

You'll want to send your letter in this packaging, rather than a regular envelope, as it will garner greater attention and set you apart from other applicants.

Things to Avoid

Professional coaches recommend a variety of post-interview strategies. I'm not a big fan of using these, but I will mention them here.

- Some candidates have sent balloons to the person(s) they interviewed with an attached message: "I'm up in the air without having a positive decision to work for your company." Unless the culture of the company is very creative and "loose/non-corporate," I would advise against this.
- Other candidates have sent gifts or a fruit basket to an interviewer's home address. I would steer clear as it smacks of stalking a person outside their work location.
- Don't send your interviewer a lotto ticket. Yes, some candidates have reportedly thought it would bring them luck. In the end, they didn't get the job, nor did they win the lottery.
- Avoid sending a shoe to "get your foot in the door" to the interviewer. This usually backfires and results in not acquiring the job offer.

When You Do Get the Offer

When you finally receive your first offer (of what I hope will be many), I suggest approaching your response with humility and gratitude.

By all means, make absolutely certain the offer meets with your budget and industry-standard salaries listed earlier in this book. Be comprehensive and fully understand the scope of your responsibilities as an employee, including—but not being limited to—any probationary periods, special assignments, requirements, etc.

If necessary, negotiate your offer with the most positive of attitudes and in good faith. You want to portray an *earnest sense of willingness* when negotiating. Remember to convey your desire to work hard for an increase in responsibilities, wages, and benefits.

Here is a secret trick to remember to use *BEFORE YOU ACCEPT* any job:

- Make certain that, in order to prove and gauge your worthiness to the company, there is a **clear path to advancement** for your position. You can do this by requesting regularly occurring employee reviews (annually, semi-annually, or quarterly). In doing so, you make certain that you are meeting your employer's benchmarks and documenting your success on a regularly occurring basis.

The purpose of this is to ensure that, from day one of your employment, if you've met your requirements, along with any other measurements that might trigger a bonus, etc., you will *actually receive* those rewards and advancements.

Subsequently, additional and precise follow-on goals and bonuses should be delineated for advancement—for the following year (or corresponding time period). Again, these should also be memorialized in writing and scheduled for your next review.

So go negotiate and solidify the offer for employment that you've worked so diligently to acquire. Congratulations!

Step #8 — Lifelong Learning

Just when you thought you were done—well—you're never really done.

In music and entertainment careers, where technology often plays a significant role in the creative process, hardware and software often change at lightning speed.

Regardless of whether you use computers for sound, video, authoring, or administration, you'll want to stay "state of the art." This will keep you competitive with others both in and outside of the workplace. It is particularly crucial to remain current if you intend to climb the corporate ladder.

It is, however, not enough to be simply "up-to-date" on software, hardware, and creative processes. You'll need to be current on business practices, too. These include procedures, filings, and all things administrative and financial.

Yes, you can rely on your personal accountant for some of these items; or if you're filing simple tax forms, you can possibly depend on good accounting software.

As you ascend to greater jobs and amass wealth—or if you seek a more entrepreneurial career—I strongly suggest retaining the services of an excellent attorney and/or financial managers. They will help you make certain that your employment agreements, tax liabilities (both professional and personal), billing practices, and payment systems are current.

From an employment standpoint, you may need to invest in *yourself*. This means:

- *Enrolling* in professional, online courses and curriculum to ensure you're knowledgeable about the latest systems, software, and applications to compete in your industry.
- *Subscribing* to and *scouring* business-to-business journals and professional publications so you become knowledgeable about industry practices, career trends, and professional standards.
- *Attending* trade conferences, certification, and continuing education programs to ensure that your prior education commitment, license, etc. remain valid and up-to-date.
- Remember that if it's something you love as much as your career, you should be prepared to continue to learn how to do what you love—for the rest of your life!

Step #9 — Be a Contrarian

Of all the ten tips...this is my absolute favorite.

For without being a contrarian, I would never have started—nor would I have continued—to earn the successes I've enjoyed in multiple careers.

So what does it mean to be a contrarian?

The dictionary defines the word *contrarian* as either:

1. A person who opposes or rejects popular opinion, especially in the stock exchange or financial dealings; or

2. Someone who goes against a current practice.

While I'm not an expert, advisor, or mentor in monetary practices, I have done my best to perfect being a contrarian in my current and former careers.

Specifically:

- A majority of my classmates moved to Los Angeles, New York, or other music centers within the United States—I located to Chicago.
- My contemporaries hunted for jobs in recording, film, television, and broadcast studios—I sought a career in professional audio equipment manufacturing, specifically in design and sales.

- Fellow career-mates switched from studio to equipment sales—I migrated to publishing, specifically selling advertisements and developing editorials in two distinct business-to-business journals for the recording studio and commercial sound and video industry.

Time and again, I have *consistently* gone against the grain in my careers, even when it was viewed as haphazard and unpopular.

For example, before anyone knew what the internet was—my wife and I launched what would become the third largest internet consultancy in the Southeastern United States. Initially, our small company of three employees performed digital marketing and traditional advertising (e.g., radio, TV, print, and online) for Fortune 100 companies.

While this move may have seemed unrelated to the music and entertainment industry, I would not have been able to retain clients like DirecTV, Sony Music, Blockbuster Entertainment, and others without my prior career experiences.

So when you think about your career—my suggestion is to THINK DIFFERENTLY.

Doing so will not always be easy or popular.

Being a contrarian, however, will be rewarding if you do it correctly. Though you needn't take my word for it:

- Apple Computer's late co-founder, chairman, and CEO Steve Jobs insisted that the word "different" should be used as a *noun*. Jobs believed phrases like "think beauty," "think victory," and "think different" all had the same usage and spirit.

And so it is in *his* spirit that I offer you the following *15 Tips to Succeeding as a Contrarian*. My hope is that you can be, think, and "succeed different."

15 Tips to Succeeding as a Contrarian

1. *Educate* Different—Don't attend a college or an online certification course because everyone else is doing the same. Find the best course for you.

2. *Locate* Different—You don't need to join the masses in big cities. Find the best location for you to excel.

3. *Career* Different—Don't settle for a job that large groups of applicants are focused on.

4. *Search* Different—Expand your search beyond the conventional and typical online methods. Meet with people, both in professional group settings and one-on-one at prospective places of employment.

5. *Solo v. Assistance* Different—People like to help others. Ask for support, and when it is your turn to provide for others, do not think twice... help them, too! Don't go it alone.

6. *Interview* Different—You needn't dress up in a clown outfit when interviewing. Instead of approaching your interviews like every other candidate, determine how you can best make a contribution to the company and the interviewer. Think about service first, and the job offer should follow.

7. *Resume* Different—Create a resume that speaks to your ability to contribute to the company, industry, and the

career that you seek. Be creative *and* professional in your resume design.

8. *Operate* Different—In an industry often tinged with relaxed, vague, and detached service, govern yourself and operate in a buttoned-up, fully professional and caring manner. Do what you say you will do. Remember to put "deeds before words."

9. *Present* Different—Dress sharp. Be clean-shaven. Stay proud and confident. Your presentation will be contagious. Let it speak positive volumes about your capabilities and caring.

10. *Be Fanatically Polite*—You can never be *too* polite. I am not talking about kissing someone's derrière. I am strongly suggesting that a "Sir," "Ma'am," "Thank you," "You're welcome," and other well-mannered and respectful phrases can take you further than being impolite, unrefined, and vulgar.

11. *Under-Promise and Over-Deliver*—Do what you say you're going to do, but do more. Delight your constituents, co-workers, employees, and customers. Every stakeholder you come in contact with should feel *listened* to, *cared* for, and made to understand they are *your top priority*.

12. *Be Early*—It is not enough to be "on time." Show up early. Stay late. Put in the extra effort. You'll get noticed and may be justly rewarded for the same. Best of all, you'll feel good about doing a thorough job.

13. *Come In Under Budget*—It's not enough to provide your deliverables on time. You should also strive to come in "under budget." As more of your coworkers and competitors likely over-spend and under-deliver, you can

turn heads, earn more business, and garner loyal fans by spending less of your customers' money and giving them deliverables faster. Be efficient!

14. *Work Harder Than Your Competition*—It goes without saying that you may be battling others throughout your career. Doing so does not need to be disrespectful or offensive. Simply work harder, smarter, faster, and more efficiently. Let your actions speak for you. Your customers, bosses, and the market may beat a path to your door.

15. *Be a Big Fish in a Small Pond*—There is nothing wrong with practicing your craft in a smaller city. The competition is likely to be less fierce, and your ability to rise to the top becomes that much easier. Remember that happiness isn't always achieved by relocating to a large metropolis. Consider becoming a big deal in a small town.

Step #10 — Before Making
A Career Change

For the moment, I would like you to turn your mind to the future.

Fast-forward your imagination five years from now. Looking ahead can be useful if you are currently in a steady career, particularly if you are not working at a job you would consider a perfect fit.

Why?

Because whether you're a student or working another job, there are serious considerations you should make before you jump ship to a new career.

Put simply...

Q.: Is switching careers or jobs always a good idea?

A.: The answer is "definitely not."

Here's why:

You may not want to leave your current job if you are presently failing. It's always better to be working at the top of your game before you leave.

Similarly, don't embark on a new career if you don't have the finances to support yourself. This is particularly important while you are in school or networking to a new career. Make sure your savings are in order.

Above all else, if you have not adequately identified what new skills you need, what type of business you want to be in, what outcome you desire, what culture you want to be with, what challenges you want to overcome, and what type of compensation is acceptable— you will not want to embark on any new job search.

Remember too that money can't buy happiness
If currently employed and your salary is the only reason causing you to seek a career change, you may want to rethink a move. Keep in mind that your happiness and ability to make contributions to others should always remain at the forefront of your career decisions.

Most career advisors suggest that your well-being is more important than your salary.

Why?

Multiple surveys indicate that most people would gladly stay at their jobs if they truly *enjoyed* their work.

But if you are constantly upset with your assignments, your work associates, or your customers—you may, in fact, be at the wrong job.

If this is the case, make certain that you have developed the skills required for a new career. You will also need a solid exit strategy to get from your current to your new job.

Developing the right network of professionals, groups, and mentors will be extremely useful. I strongly suggest you accomplish this well before leaving your present job.

Is Jumping Ship the Right Choice?

To recapitulate, here's a solid checklist to help you decide.

Don't Leave Your Current Situation if You...
- Are failing at your career.
- Do not have the finances or education needed.
- Have not defined what new skills are required.
- Have not mastered those skills.
- Have not identified what type of new business to be in.
- Have not defined what outcome you want.
- Have not located the right culture to be with.
- Have not defined what challenges you want.
- Have not identified an acceptable compensation level.

Do Leave Your Current Circumstances if...
- Your salary is not the only lever causing you to seek a change.
- You are unhappy at your current job.
- You are upset with the type of work and tasks you perform.
- Your performance reviews are indicative of your unhappiness and lack of productivity.

Before Embarking on a New Move, Make Sure You Have...
- The right skills for a new career.
- A solid strategy to exit from your current to new career.

- The right network, mentors, and experts to help you.

Consider Working with a Career Coach or a Mentor Who Has...

- Great familiarity with the music and entertainment industry.
- A track record of success within the career sector you are seeking.
- Experience advising others and who has her/his own multi-faceted career in music and entertainment industries.
- The expertise to provide you value by shrinking the time, dollars, and effort necessary to produce a return on your investment.

Run Around Your Backhand

In tennis, players who don't have a solid backhand shot often run out of their way to hit every ball with their forehand. This is called "running around your backhand."

While you *can* certainly play tennis this way, it's *extremely inefficient*.

Imagine the extra exertion required to play like this. You expend up to 100% more effort than if you were equally comfortable hitting backhand shots. It is simply not sustainable to play with such a critical missing component.

The metaphor holds true for business and career development as well, and here's why:

- If you're not good at something that needs attention, admit it and get assistance.
- If it's a personality issue, attend to it.

- If it's a group dynamic, work things out—seek professional assistance with a coach, mentor, or with psychological/medical expertise.
- If it's a performance, knowledge, or technical issue—increase your learning capacity and learn what needs to be in your toolkit.

Doing so will put you in an advantageous position.

Except those who are forced into continuing educational compliance, few if any employees show the initiative to pursue a lifelong learning of their craft. Those who work on their personality and ability to improve work cultures are even fewer in number.

Managers, senior personnel, human resources will notice you. Moreover, they are likely to fight for your advancement at your job.

You will also be better prepared when and if you do switch careers because you'll have a track record of growth, sustainability, and proof that you are always up to learning more about yourself, your craft, and those around you.

Chapter 4
Summary

Life isn't about finding yourself.
Life is about creating yourself.

- George Bernard Shaw

If you've skipped to this part of the book hoping to "short-cut" the *Ten Essential Steps Necessary to Succeed in the Music or Entertainment Industry*, I am sorry to report the there are no CliffsNotes™, alternatives, or time-saving methods.

Regrettably, you're just going to have to read the book and do the work.

On the other hand, if you've arrived at the page after reviewing all of the information prior to this chapter...I congratulate you.

And if you've taken actionable steps and have moved closer to achieving your goal, picture this: I'm standing up and applauding you.

Really...I hope that you will take a moment to let me know what you've done. Send me an email, or communicate with me on social media.

Bottom line is this... in order to ensure your success, you should:

1. *Identify* the career you want in the industry.

2. *Research* specifics about career opportunities that match up with the career you've defined.

3. *Locate and speak* to employers and organizations who are hiring.

4. *Create* deliverables that differentiate you from other candidates, and make sure they are meaningful to your target organization.

5. *Participate* in professional groups and meet with industry leaders to create a wider career network.

6. *Interview* and determine how you can make a contribution to your prospective employer.

7. *Follow up*, negotiate terms, and gauge your success through regularly scheduled employee reviews.

8. *Educate* yourself through a lifelong learning process.

9. *Carve* your own unique path to success by being a contrarian.

10. *Analyze* your rationale and preparedness before making career changes.

If you attend to each of the ten steps above and apply the detailed information provided in this book, you have the capacity to achieve a variety of successes as I have done in multiple careers.

While nothing in this world is guaranteed, I have found that people who work efficiently, with an accompanying strategy and network of professional and diligent application of their skills, succeed more often than those who simply meander through their professional and personal lives.

I did it.

I believe you can do it.

I wish you only the very best of success in your efforts, strategy, and diligence.

Chapter 5
Endnotes and Offers

"Kindness is the language
the deaf can hear and
the blind can see."
- *Mark Twain*

This could be one of the most important chapters in the book.

Why?

Because, in addition to providing you with a variety of FREE tools and resources to use in your search for the ultimate music or entertainment industry career, it also provides you with a clear path to contacting me and engaging my services to help you—both in group settings and privately if you so desire.

While you are certainly not required to keep in touch with me, I welcome you to do so. Even if you drop me a line and tell me what was helpful and what was not, I would truly enjoy hearing from you.

In that way, I can refine my methodology and make certain to help more people as efficiently and correctly as possible.

So how do you contact me?

You Can Reach Me at...
Either of the following websites:

- www.davidruttenberg.com
- www.MusiCareers.com

You can also find my **blog** here.

I'm all over **social media** too, including Facebook, Twitter (or @HiMusiCareers), YouTube, LinkedIn, Google+, Pinterest, and Reddit.

And, of course, you can **email** me at Hello@MusiCareers.com, or call any time at +1 (415) 723-0562. Yes...that's my telephone number, and I'd love to hear from you, particularly if you want to hire me as your personal mentor/coach, lecturer, producer, engineer/mixer, or composer/arranger.

What About More Free Stuff?

I am glad you asked.

I have curated a short but powerful set of "Freebies" for you to get your hands on below. From checklist to flash bulletins to new book announcements—even a contest to win a free mentoring session with me—they are listed below.

Make sure you sign up right now.

- **10 Things You Need to Know to SUCCEED in the Music Business Today Checklist**—If you haven't downloaded this, it is the perfect companion to this book. You can get it by clicking here.
- **Flash Bulletin**—Periodically, I post secret, hidden job and career opportunities inside my *MusiCareers Flash Bulletin*. If you'd like to know about these, along with other special forthcoming giveaways, new free e-books (the next in this series), mentoring programs, free webinars or teleconferences, you can sign up here. About once a month, whenever new job postings become available, you'll receive a *Flash Bulletin* email.
- **New Book Announcement**—Did you know that the book you're reading is Part One in a series of e-books that I've

authored? As new books become available, a certain number of free downloads are allotted for readers like you. Sign up here to be included.

- **Free Mentor Session Contest**—Once a month, I provide a free, 1-hour mentoring session to a lucky winner. Just sign up here and you'll automatically be entered to win. No purchase necessary.

One More Thing...A Small Favor:

I want to thank you for allowing me the opportunity to share these pages with you. If you found this book useful, I have a small favor to ask:

If you have a moment, would you please leave a review to my Amazon book page? Doing so will not only help me continue to write more books in this series, it will let others know that you found the information useful. Just click here after you've signed into your Amazon account. That way, your review will be a **verified** review (very important).

In advance of your review, I thank you...and as always, I wish you the very best in your search for the perfect job and career in the music and entertainment industry.

About The Author

"I've never walked the same path
other people found comfortable
and I'm not going to start now."

- Lora Leigh

As a sustaining member of the GRAMMYs®, Broadcast Music International (BMI), the American Federal of Musicians (AFM), and the Recording Industry Association of America (RIAA), David Ruttenberg has been fortunate to work with A-list entertainers and up-and-coming stars—including some of the biggest names in the entertainment and business world: Peter Gabriel, Stevie Wonder, Janet Jackson, Lindsey Buckingham, 3M, DirecTV, Goodyear Tire and Rubber, and Blockbuster Video.

Prior to serving as a GRAMMY® producer—AFM engineer/mixer—BMI composer/arranger/publisher, Ruttenberg honed his business acumen serving in upper-level posts of companies including NEOTEK Corporation, Otari Corporation, *Recording-Engineer-Producer (REP) Magazine*, *Sound & Video Contractor (S&VC) Magazine*, and GATE International.

David has produced, engineered, and mastered thousands of tracks and has completed project work for Jeff Berlin, Russ Freeman, The Rippingtons, and Eric Marienthal. In the process, Ruttenberg's work has been featured alongside tracks performed by Chick Corea, Peter Erskine, and Russell Ferrante.

David also spends time raising awareness and money for charitable causes, including the Margaux's Miracle Foundation through Memorial Sloan Kettering Cancer Center's Pediatric Department. He's created two smooth-jazz solo albums—*Sunset Key* and *Miracles*—specifically for these causes.

Ruttenberg mastered his performance, engineering, and production skills by attending both the George Washington

University and the University of Miami. He has degrees from the latter's Frost School of Music and College of Engineering.

David lectures at many colleges and universities and provides private instruction and mentoring to clients both in his Florida studio and online. His clients describe his easygoing style as friendly, humorous, and balanced by a love of all things technical and creative.

He is equally at home in recording, mixing, and mastering studios, working on major and independent projects. You can contact David Ruttenberg directly at hello@MusiCareers.com or at +1 (415) 723-0562.

Made in the USA
Middletown, DE
25 April 2019